MEDALLION QUILTS

OTHER BOOKS BY JINNY BEYER

Patchwork Patterns

The Quilter's Album of Blocks and Borders

JINNY BEYER

THE ART AND TECHNIQUE
OF CREATING

MEDALLION QUILTS

INCLUDING A RICH COLLECTION
OF CONTEMPORARY AND
HISTORIC EXAMPLES

EPM PUBLICATIONS, INC.

EPM Publications, Inc.
1003 Turkey Run Road
McLean, Virginia 22101

Printed in the United States of America

LIBRARY OF CONGRESS CATALOGING IN PUBLICATION DATA
Beyer, Jinny.
   Medallion quilts.
   Subtitle: The art and technique of creating medallion
quilts, including a rich collection of historic and
contemporary examples.
   Bibliography: p.
   Includes index.
   1. Quilting. I. Title.
TT835.B427 1982   746.9'7   82-13744
ISBN 0-939009-02-1

Illustrations: Jinny Beyer and Dan Ramsey
Photography: Steve Tuttle
Design: Christina Lego

Jacket Photograph: Blue Star Sapphire,
pieced medallion quilt by Jinny Beyer

Contents

The designs in this book have been labeled according to the categories developed in Mrs. Beyer's previous two books. The plastic grid from *The Quilter's Album of Blocks and Borders* can be used to help understand how to draft these designs.

List of Photographs

Acknowledgments

I wish to express my sincere thanks to the many people who contributed to the production of this book. Several museum and historical societies gave their time and knowledge and aided me in obtaining photographs of quilts from their respective collections. Many individuals helped me by giving their time, talents or allowing me to use photographs of their quilts.

Special thanks go to Dan Ramsey, who once again did a superb job of illustrating, to Steve Tuttle, whose expertise has captured the workmanship and beauty of each quilt he photographed, and to Barbara Bockman, Betty Larson, Judy Spahn and Bonnie Stratton for their help during the final stages of the book.

Institutions
Jean Federico, Curator of Textiles, and Gloria Allen, The Daughters of the American Revolution Museum, Washington, D.C.; Imelda G. DeGraw, Curator of Textiles, The Denver Art Museum, Denver, Colorado; Christine Meadows, Curator, and Nancy J. Emison, Assistant Curator, The Mount Vernon Ladies' Association of the Union, Mount Vernon, Virginia; Philadelphia Museum of Art, Philadelphia, Pennsylvania; Bob Shaw, Shelburne Museum, Shelburne, Vermont; Doris Bowman, Curator of Textiles, and Joan Stevens, The Smithsonian Institution, Washington D.C., Barbara Naef, Sully Plantation, Fairfax County Park Authority, Virginia.

Collectors
Pat McLaughlin, Virginia; Sandra Mitchell, Southfield, Michigan; Linda Reuther, San Rafael, California; Merry and Al Silber, Birmingham, Michigan; Julie Silber, San Rafael, California.

Quiltmakers and Historians
Mary Albright, North Carolina; Boots Bartell, Virginia; Lena Behme, Virginia; Cuesta Benberry, Missouri; Ellie Bennett, Pennsylvania; Barbara S. Bockman, Hazel Carter, Virginia; Joan Christianson, Virginia; Alice Geiger, Virginia; Fay Goldey, Maryland; Colleen Gosling, Virginia; Mary Granger, Tennessee; Joyce Gross, California; Connie Gunn, Virginia;

Linda Hause, Maryland; Louise Hayes, Virginia; Nancy Johnson, Maryland; Eleanor Kastner, Virginia; Barbara Kirkconnell, Maryland; Katherine Kuhn, Virginia; Kathy Lane, Maryland; Betty Larson, Virginia; Lois Lightfoot, Virginia; Carolyn Lynch, Virginia; Pat Madlener, Virginia; Anne McClintic, Pennsylvania; Susan McKelvey, Maryland; Pat McLaughlin, Virginia; Yoko Sawanabori, Maryland; Darlene Shumway, Virginia; Mary Ellen Simmons, Virginia; Diane Smith, Maryland; Judy Spahn, Virginia; Virginia Suzuki, Virginia; Ellen Swanson, Virginia; Jean Timken, Maryland; Marilyn Titman, Virginia; Sandy Tucker, Maryland; Audrey Waite, Germany; Gail Wentzel, Virginia; P.J. Wormington, Virginia.

I wish also to thank the many students of mine who have given me inspiration and knowledge.

Photographs not credited to a museum or individual have been made by Steve Tuttle of Photo Works West, Alexandria, Virginia.

Preface

The medallion quilt, known for its ornamental center pattern surrounded by borders, reached the height of its glory during the latter part of the 18th century. Its popularity was most likely linked to the styles of fabrics that were being imported into Europe and America from India. As the years went by, other forms of quiltmaking became more popular. Now with modern-day quilters paying even more attention to design and color continuity than their 18th century predecessors, however, we are experiencing a rebirth of interest in medallion quilts. Today's quiltmakers look for ways to repeat pattern, color, fabric and borders to achieve a totally unified effect. The medallion quilt is not an "accident" but a carefully planned design.

My own interest in medallion quilts also stems from Indian influences. Two years of living in India in 1970–72 had a great impact on me. The wealth of color, pattern, design and borders was everywhere—in the dress of the Indians, in their home decor and in their buildings as well. I became fascinated with the rich fabrics accented by decorative borders, and the ornate structures with inlaid, free-flowing floral motifs. All that I saw impressed me deeply and has influenced my approach to the use of color and borders in my quilt designs.

This book sets forth concepts for medallion quilt construction and design derived both from my personal quiltmaking and teaching. The teaching experience has continuously generated new thoughts and ideas about medallion quilts, my own designs and those of my students. I have learned far more from students than I have taught them. This book has come about now only because after conducting many medallion quilt classes and seeing and working with examples, I have been able to formulate certain thoughts about this type of quilt. These are not "rules" that one must live by but rather concepts that *seem* to add to the success of the whole quilt. These ideas are not something I have always known. I have many more ideas today about what may work successfully than when I taught my first medallion class. Next year there will be even more ideas which I will wish were included here.

This is not a pattern book. Patterns for medallion quilts would tend to stifle creativity and prevent experimentation and growth. Every person harbors a spark of originality. What I have endeavored to do here is to kindle the spark, to offer those guidelines and suggestions for medallion quilt design that will enable you to draw upon your own experiences and ideas and to create a quilt that is uniquely your own.

THE ART AND TECHNIQUE

OF CREATING

MEDALLION

QUILTS

INCLUDING A RICH COLLECTION

OF CONTEMPORARY AND

HISTORIC EXAMPLES

Historical Development

Framed center, framed medallion, central medallion—all these are terms that have historically referred to the type of quilt that has a central motif surrounded by a series of borders. One cannot simply date the earliest medallion quilts and assume that their history began at that point. In order to understand why quilts were made in a particular style, it is necessary to know the trends in fashion, industry, and the politics and economics of the times.

The height of medallion quiltmaking, prior to the present day, seems to have been reached in the late 18th and early 19th centuries. How did the style begin and why was it so popular?

Perhaps it began in the 1500s when, using the newly discovered route around the Cape of Good Hope, the first Portuguese traders sailed to India and found quilts and painted cloths, which they called *pintados* (Portuguese for *pinta*, meaning "spot" or "fleck"). These were unlike anything they had ever seen. The few pieces of fabrics that made their way back to Europe aroused great curiosity and were regarded as novelties because they were completely different from anything heretofore available.

This fabric, with its decorative motifs and borders, came to be known as "chintz." Today one thinks of chintz as a glazed, plain or floral, cotton fabric used mostly for draperies or upholstery. In India it was the name given to painted or printed cloth, some of which was glazed. The name is derived from Hindi *chitta* meaning "spotted cloth." It appeared in numerous English records as "chint" (singular) or "chints" (plural)—with other variations as "cit," "chit," "chites," "cheetes," "schite." These fabrics were also referred to as "pintados" and "palampores" (in Hindi, *palamposh*, derived from Persian and Hindi *palangposh*, meaning "bed cover").

As the Dutch and English became involved in trade with the East and established East India companies in 1597 and 1600 respectively, the importance of the Indian cloth grew. Trade was initially begun to obtain the valuable spices that for centuries had been a much coveted commodity. As early as the 13th century, individual peppercorns were used as

Painted cotton Indian prayer rug made into a child's quilt. Early 19th century. (Courtesy of the Smithsonian Institution, Washington D.C.)

currency to pay taxes and purchase foods. If a bride were lucky, she would receive a dowry of pepper.

> "By the late Middle Ages oriental spices were valued roughly as follows: A pound of saffron cost the same as a horse; a pound of ginger as much as a sheep; two pounds of mace would buy a cow. . . . When one considers the wretched victuals of 15th century Europe it is easy to understand the extraordinary value placed on spices. . . . In an epoch when Europe knew nothing of sugar, tea, coffee, chocolate, potatoes, citrus fruits or tobacco, to say nothing of plumbing or refrigeration, Oriental spices supplied flavor and piquancy for food and drink and fragrant aromas to mask a multitude of unpleasant odors. . . . So useful, indeed indispensable, were spices that kings sent expeditions in search of them, merchants risked life and fortune to trade in them, wars were fought over them."[1]

The high cost of spices was due to the tedious process of getting them to Europe. The only known way to reach the orient was the overland route through the Middle East; thus the Arabs developed a monopoly on the trade. "After leaving the hands of the native producers, the spices passed through numerous dealers before they reached the markets of the Black Sea and the Eastern Mediterranean, and with each change of ownership came an addition to the cost."[2]

With such a high premium placed on spices, once a ship route was discovered, the Europeans were anxious to establish direct trade with the islands of the Malay archipelago, known as the Spice Islands. The people of the Islands had no need for European currency, so it was necessary for traders to find a commodity with which to barter. The English attempted to trade their woolens (which were in abundant supply), but they were met with little interest in such a hot climate. The people of the Islands wanted lightweight, bright-colored Indian cottons, which had been brought to them earlier by Arab traders. So the triangle of trade was set up: The ships went around the Cape of Good Hope, up to India to buy cottons, from there to the Malay archipelago to trade the cottons for spices, and then back around the Cape and home to Europe. The trip was long and arduous. Scurvy and other diseases were rampant on the ships, and many lives were lost on each voyage.

Each ship that returned to England would bring a few Indian quilts and pieces of cloth. "The first India cottons came to England as 'token' parcels on heavily-laden spice ships. They were intended as something special for the Directors, [executives of the East India Company] or as bribery items rather than commodities. Everbody *seized* upon them."[3]

[1]Frederic Rosengarten, Jr., *The Book of Spices* (Wynnewood, Pa.: Livingston Publishing Co., 1969); pp. 47–48.

[2]John W. Parry, *The Story of Spices* (New York: Chemical Publishing Co., 1953) p. 83.

[3]John Irwin, "Origins of the 'Oriental Style' in English Decorative Art," *Burlington Magazine* 96 (1959): p. 108.

No painted or printed cotton was available anywhere in Europe at that time. The fabrics in existence were damasks, velvets, wools, silk, heavy tapestries or plain household linens. "Velvets, brocades, and damasks then in fashion contained either large symmetrical designs of highly stylized flowers and foliage, or small repeated patterns of geometric forms or stiff little leaf sprigs. The Indian designs in contrast were alive with free naturalistic movement, the floral forms full of fantasy, the colors brilliant."[4] Any printing on cotton being done in Europe was primitive and crude, and the cloth was not colorfast. It was the brilliance and fastness of the colors that gave the Indian cloth some of its greatest appeal. In fact, the colors seemed to improve with washing. However, there is no factual evidence of this, and it "doubtless arose from the simple observation of the colours of a dirty fabric seeming brighter after removal of the dirt."[5]

The early Indian fabrics were designed not to appeal to European tastes but to please Islamic patrons with whom India was currently trading. The fabrics also met needs of the Indians themselves—for clothing, tent hangings, prayer rugs, cloths for sitting, and some quilts and bed covers (palampores). These cloths had beautiful floral patterns and borders, and many of the designs were influenced by the Persians, who had recently established their presence in India. However, the dark background of most of the fabric was contrary to European taste.

> "The characteristic seventeenth-century [Indian] palampore and quilt designs comprised a central medallion and four related corner motifs on a flowery field surrounded by a wide border. The ultimate source of the medallion and corner motifs was probably . . . Persian which may also be said to have inspired the same elements in Persian carpet-design."[6]

These Indian palampores were to have an immense impact on European and American quilt design.

Extensive study of the East India Company's documents, company letters and records has been done by John Irwin, Katharine Brett and Alice Beer in research for their respective books and articles. Much of their information on the trade of cottons was obtained from India Office records of the East India Company. As early as 1613 the directors of the Company coveted the few fabrics that reached Europe and lamented the fact that there were not enough to sell. They inquired about whether or not the fabrics would be successful as commodities, but there is no record of the response to the inquiry. Not until 1643 did the next reference occur in the Company's documents concerning the sale of

[4]Katharine Brett, "Chintz, an Influence of the East on the West," *Antiques* 64 (Dec. 1953): p. 481.

[5]John Irwin and Katharine Brett, *Origins of Chintz* (London: Her Majesty's Stationery Office, 1970), p. 1.

[6]Ibid., p. 27.

Indian chintz, when in the East Indian Company's London auction

> "'Pintadoe Quilts' fetched 50s. each. This was considered a disappointing price and prompted the directors to comment that 'they serve more to content and pleasure our friends than for any profit (that) ariseth in sales, your first cost, freight and custom being all put together . . . 60 or 100 quilts will be as many as one year will want. Those which here-after you shall send we desire may be with more white ground, and the flowers and branch to be in colours in the middle of the quilt as the painter pleases, whereas now the most part of your quilts come with sad red grounds which are not equally sorted to please all buyers."[7]

This may well be the first example of an English request for Indian cloth to conform more to the European taste. As mentioned in the quotation above, a lighter ground was preferable to the "sad red grounds" of the materials they had been receiving. Perhaps it was the response to such requests that caused a dramatic increase in the demand for the cloth. Around 1660, orders suddenly jumped from 100 pieces per shipment to 14,000.[8] In 1662 the East India Company sent actual patterns for the Indians to copy, and by the late 1600s, demand for the fabric became overwhelming. More and more the cloth was being ordered to meet English specifications—not only according to color but eventually to design and size. The elaborately outfitted bed was an important piece of furniture and the English were requesting fabrics from India specifically suited for bed fittings. In fact, as early as 1683 an order was sent to the East India Company from London for

> "100 Suits of painted Curtaines and Vallances, made ready up of Several Sorts and Prices. The Vallances to be 1 foot deep and 6½ yards compass. Curtains to be from 8 to 9 foot deep, the lesser Curtains each 1½ yds wide, the two larger Curtains to be 3½ yds wide. The Tester and headpiece pro-porceonable. A Counterpane of the same work to be 3½ yds wide and 4 yds long half of them to be quilted and the other half not quilted."[9]

A fashion trend favoring Chinese art had already developed in Europe. Consequently, some of the European designs that were sent to India had a Chinese flair. These were never exactly copied but were interpreted by the Indians in their own way, thus providing an interesting mixture of East and West and creating an exotic look that captured the fancy of all of Europe.

> "Designs copied by the Indian cotton-painters from English patterns had by this time become so parodied that by the time they reached England their European origin was often

---

[7]Ibid., pp. 3-4.

[8]John Irwin, "Origins of 'Oriental' Chintz Design," *Antiques* 75 (Jan. 1959): p. 85.

[9]Irwin and Brett, *Origins of Chintz*, p. 25.

Palampore with typical tree of life design from the Goa area in west central India. 18th century. 84″ x 120″. (Courtesy of the Denver Art Museum, Denver, Colorado.)

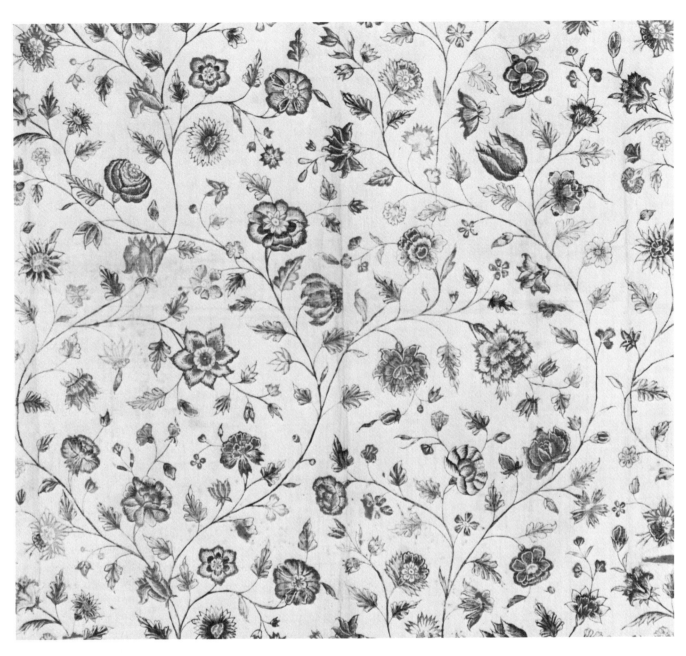

Indian chintz detail, showing the free-flowing floral pattern typical of the Indian fabrics. Mid–18th century. 21″ x 22″. (Courtesy of the Smithsonian Institution, Washington D.C.)

unrecognised. English and Chinese flowers, distorted into something fanciful by Indian eyes to whom the plants were alien, were now welcomed in their new form as expressions of exotic fantasy. The wheel had turned full circle. What had earlier been sent out to help the Indian craftsmen to conform to conventions of English taste were now returning in parodied form to feed the new appetite for exoticism. The directors wanted more and more of such goods, and the more fanciful the better!"[10]

By the end of the 17th century a definite pattern had been established in the desire for Indian goods. "By far the most numerous references in the East Indian Company records were for quilts and palampores".[11]

[10]Ibid., p. 5.
[11]Ibid., p. 26

On February 16, 1669, the London directors of the East India Company wrote to their agents at Surat:

> "Now of late, they are here in England, come to a great practize of printing large branches for Hangings of Romes, And we doe believe, yet some of our Callicoes, painted after that manner might vent well, and therefore have sent you some patternes, of which wee would have you send us 2000 pieces in the sorte and quantities foll:. . . . Send us also 100 Quilts of the same workes, with hansome large Borders."[12]

There were basically two patterns of Indian chintz. One variety was the tree of life designs, and although the details were depicted a thousand different ways, they were composed of a tree growing on a mound with birds, butterflies, exotic flowers, animals and sometimes human figures. These were surrounded by a "wide floral border and a narrow inner border of tiny flower sprigs."[13] The tree of life is an ancient symbol based on "the age old conception of the Tree of Knowledge of Good and Evil in Paradise."[14] A symbol from Biblical times in the Garden of Eden and in Greek and Hindu mythology, it became stylized in many cultures. In oriental art it symbolized life eternal. The Persians added their influence to the Indian design of the tree before the Europeans ever reached India, and then when the Europeans sent their own patterns for "branched hangings" (with the Chinese flair that was then stylish in Europe), the design was further stylized. Thus the early flowering tree designs show an intermingling of Persian, Indian, European and Chinese influences.

The second type of Indian chintz had borders around the outer edges similar to the flowering tree. However, the central area had an all-over design of flowers.[15] The tree of life designs, floral patterns and the repeated use of borders found in these Indian fabrics had a great impact on early medallion quilt design.

Soon there was such widespread use of the Indian cottons that the demand far exceeded the supply. Chintz was used on beds, on walls, for curtains and for clothing. It was everywhere. Daniel Defoe, the English novelist and journalist, produced his own periodical, *The Review*, from 1704 to 1713. He was often outspoken concerning politics and economics. In the January 31, 1708, edition he had this to say about the Indian goods:

> "The general fansie of the people runs upon East India goods to that degree that the 'chintz' and 'painted callicoes', which before were only made use of for carpets, quilts, &c, and to clothe children and ordinary people, become now the dress of our ladies; and such is the power of a mode we saw our

---

[12]Ibid., p. 4.

[13]Brett, "Chintz," p. 481.

[14]Pamela Clabburn, *The Needleworker's Dictionary* (New York: William Morrow & Co., 1976), p. 270.

[15]Brett, "Chintz," p. 481.

Hand-painted and quilted Indian palampore, with tree of life design. Second quarter, 18th century. The following inscription is in the upper left corner: "(Love Talk) This quilt was purchased 1736 of a smuggler of East Indian goods in the Isle of White England. Belonging to my late friend Miss Bradford. Elizabeth Smith Charleston." 86½″ x 113″. (Courtesy of the Smithsonian Institution, Washington D.C.)

Detail of the painted and quilted Indian palampore shown opposite. (Courtesy of the Smithsonian Institution, Washington D.C.)

persons of quality dressed in Indian carpets, which but a few years before their chambermaids would have thought too ordinary for them: the chintz was advanced from lying upon their floors to their backs, from the foot-cloth to the petticoat; and even the queen herself at this time was pleased to appear in China and Japan; I mean China silks and callico. Nor was this all, but it crept into our houses, our closets, and bed-chambers; curtains, cushions, chairs, and at last beds themselves were nothing but callicoes or Indian stuffs; and in short, almost everything that used to be made of wool or silk, relating either to the dress of the women or the furniture of our houses, was supplied by the Indian trade."[16]

The Indian cloth was expensive, due partly to the demand but also to the tedious process of making it, coupled with the long and hard voyage around the Cape of Good Hope. Obviously, producing cloth at home would be considerably cheaper; mills and printing plants began to spring up turning out imitations of the imported goods. Wanting to profit from the popularity of the Indian fabrics, European manufacturers called their product "indiennes," and the style showed a definite Indian influence. Soon the woolen and silk industries of England and France respectively were seriously jeopardized.

More and more the fashions of the day dictated the use of chintz in clothing and furnishings. In 1686 France placed bans on the import of Indian cottons and the manufacture

[16] Daniel DeFoe, *Weekly Review*, Jan. 31, 1708, in Edward Baines, *History of the Cotton Manufacture in Great Britain* (London: H. Fisher, R. Fisher, and P. Jackson, 1835). pp. 78-79.

of printed cottons at home, and in 1700 England followed suit. The bans, however, merely stimulated the printers in England, and some printing factories even operated secretly on protected church properties. Furthermore, it was still legal to manufacture fabrics for export and to import fabric for the purpose of reexport. Ships, supposedly sending goods to the Continent, secretly unloaded them in England. "So great was this abuse that in 1719 the Government was compelled to acknowledge that 'there are more Callicoes worn in England that pay no duty than what are painted and worn here that do pay duty. . . .'"[17] In 1720 England imposed a second ban forbidding the wearing of chintz and its use in upholstery or furnishing. This, of course, had little effect and only served to create an even greater desire for the goods. People were allowed to use cloth purchased before the ban was imposed, and who could prove whether the cloth was bought before or after? Goods were still smuggled in and also could be obtained from Holland where there was no ban. Daniel Defoe, writing again on the subject in 1728, said:

> "All the Kings and Parliaments . . . cannot govern our Fancies: They may make laws . . . for your Good; but two Things among us are too ungovernable, viz. our Passions and our Fashions. . . . SHOULD I ask the Ladies, whether they would dress by Law, they would ask me whether they were to be Statute Fools . . . whether the Parliament had nothing [better] to do. . . . [they would say] that they claim 'English' Liberty as well as the Men, and as they expect to do what they please, and say what they please, so they will wear what they please, and dress how they please."[18]

By 1774 all restrictions were removed, but their existence had put a definite crimp on trade with India, which never again reached the magnitude of the earlier times. The European textile printing industry suffered still another setback in 1789 during the French Revolution.

Because of all of these combined factors—the high cost of importing Indian fabrics, the prohibition and consequent reduction of trade with India, and the Revolution—chintz was very dear during the 1700s and not always readily available. This shortage only added lustre to the "look" of the Indian palampores with tree of life designs or floral bouquets surrounded by borders.

Quite likely for this reason, women of the 18th century began to fashion quilts in the same style. For at least two centuries, it had been a common practice in Europe to embroider decorative motifs on sturdy fabric such as linen and then to cut out and appliqué them on to a finer fabric such as silk or velvet. From the time of the Mogul takeover of Northern India in the 16th century, much of the Indian de-

[17]Irwin and Brett, *Origins of Chintz*, p. 5.

[18]Daniel DeFoe, *A Plan of the English Commerce* (Great Britain: Shakespeare Head Press, 1927), pp. 189–190.

Appliqué quilt top in "broderie perse" technique. The tree of life center is from sections of old cut chintz; the printed borders are of hand-blocked fabrics. Late 18th century, of southern origin, 93" x 96". (Courtesy of the Shelburne Museum, Shelburne, Vermont.)

Detail of quilt shown on p. 22 showing the fine buttonhole stitch that was often used to appliqué pieces of chintz to a background fabric. From the trousseau of Mary Ann Barringer who married Dr. Charles Wilson Harris on July 1, 1828. (Courtesy of the Daughters of the American Revolution Museum, Washington D.C.)

Detail of quilt top shown on p. 36 showing the still brilliant colors which John Hewson used in his hand-printed fabrics. In this piece the original Hewson print has been cut apart and appliquéd to a muslin background. (Courtesy of the Smithsonian Institution, Washington D.C.)

Penn Treaty Quilt made by Martha Washington in the last quarter of the 18th century. The central motif is a scene depicting William Penn signing with the Indians. It was printed on copperplate fabric in brown tones sometime between 1780 and 1790. The patchwork surrounding the center is typical of the relatively simple patchwork designs of the 18th century. 100¾″ square. (Courtesy of the Mount Vernon Ladies' Association of the Union, Mount Vernon, Virginia.)

Pieced and appliquéd quilt top of English chintz, probably of English origin. Some of the piecing is done in the English style of patchwork over paper. 96½″ x 104″. c. 1810. (Courtesy of the Shelburne Museum, Shelburne, Vermont.)

sign had reflected Persian influences. In fact, the emperor Akbar brought Persian embroiderers to work in India. It is likely, then, that the Europeans thought the Indian fabrics had the look of Persian embroidery, or "broderie perse." In addition, the technique of "resht" work became known in Europe. This type of needlework was used in Persia mainly for prayer rugs and saddle cloths and was made by cutting out pieces of fabric and applying them to a different colored background. The pieces were outlined by cord or chain stitch and additional details were sometimes embroidered.[19]

As the Indian cloth became expensive and scarce, women tried to copy the look and to produce a substitute for the "whole cloth" palampore spreads that had been imported from India. The techniques of "resht" work and their own embroidery and appliqué techniques, which they had been using for centuries, combined to produce what we now call "broderie perse." The majority of the earliest medallion quilts we see were made in this style by carefully cutting out birds, flowers, trees, baskets, etc., from pieces of chintz and appliquéing them onto a background fabric. The appliqué was often done with a fine buttonhole stitch. (See page 13.) Some quilts were further embellished with embroidery. *The Dictionary of Needlework* published in 1882 defined the technique as it was done at that time:

> " . . . In Broderie Perse the applied pieces are shaded and coloured pieces of chintz or cretonne, representing flowers, foliage, birds, and animals in their natural colours. These require no backing, and are simply pasted upon a coloured foundation and caught down with a Feather or open Buttonhole Stitch. . . . Stretch the background upon a frame or clothes horse, and paste the chintz flowers into position upon it. . . . When the pasting is finished and dry, take the work out of the frame and BUTTONHOLE around the leaves and flowers."[20]

Most of the "broderie perse" style quilts were made in the medallion style with a central design consisting of a flowering tree, floral motifs, urns, wreaths or baskets, surrounded by various borders. I believe this style of quiltmaking is directly related to the imported Indian chintz and in particular to the Indian fabrics known as palampores. There is no mistaking the similarities between the Indian palampore shown on page 10 and the "broderie perse" style quilts.

There is speculation that the "broderie perse" style of quiltmaking developed when people wanted to salvage used pieces of chintz, discarding those parts that had already been worn out. These bits and pieces were cut apart and appliquéd to a background fabric. I am inclined to question this assumption. Many of these quilts were considered "best" quilts and have been carefully preserved. Some ap-

[19]Clabburn, *Needleworker's Dictionary*, p. 226.
[20]S.F.A. Caulfield and Blanche Saward, *The Dictionary of Needlework, An Encyclopedia of Artistic, Plain, and Fancy Needlework* (London: L. Upcott Gill, 1882), pp. 10–11.

"Broderie perse" appliqué quilt with tree of life design reminiscent of an Indian palampore. c. 1830. 103" x 110". (Courtesy of the Smithsonian Institution, Washington D.C.)

"Broderie perse" tree of life quilt. The appliqué is cut from English block-printed cotton fabric or an Indian hand-painted palampore, and appliquéd to a handspun linen ground. Made in America, late 18th century. 106″ x 107″. (Courtesy of the Shelburne Museum, Shelburne, Vermont.)

pear never to have been washed, for they still have the glaze on the chintz. With repeated launderings, used fabric would have lost its glaze; therefore those quilts must have been made with new cloth. With the minute detail and precise workmanship on some of the quilts, it is hard to imagine that the maker would have used cloth that was already worn. More likely she used scraps left over from other sewing projects or bought fabric for these special quilts, just as we do today. With the scarcity of chintz a major factor, she may have been able to afford only a yard or two, or perhaps

17

Tree of life appliqué quilt in the "borderie perse" technique. The tree has been fabricated from pieces of chintz. Pencil lines marking the quilting can still be seen. Early 19th century. 112" x 116". (Courtesy of the Shelburne Museum, Shelburne, Vermont.)

that was all that was available. The chintz was then carefully cut apart and appliquéd to the surface of another piece of fabric, which made up the quilt top and emulated the style of the palampores. In this way a lesser amount of prized fabric could be "stretched" in the making of a whole quilt.

About the same time that England began trading with India, the first settlers were arriving in New England. Historical records show that as early as the late 17th century East Indian goods were being brought to the colonists in America. Alice Beer in her book *Trade Goods* noted several instances: The will of Margrita Van Varich taken in New York in May 1695/96 listed many Indian materials, among which were "one Chint flowered carpet, one callico Carpet, a pss. of Chints and remnant of Chints, one Chint petticote, one callico wastcote, seven chints mantells . . ." ("callico carpet" was not a carpet as we know it, but a cloth to cover furniture). The Public Records Office in London documented exports to the colonies and in 1749 listed 23 textiles, all but three of which are surely Indian, beginning with Bandannoes and ending with Palampores. *The Providence Gazette* on January 21, 1764, noted, "Smith Sabin at the Sultan's Head, near Great Bridge, hereby inform their customers that they have just received a fresh supply of European and East India Goods."[21]

It is unnecessary to reiterate here the years of hardships, struggles, and undaunted courage of the first settlers in America. By the 1700s, however, the severity of life in the colonies had eased, and all activities were not devoted solely to survival. Goods became more plentiful. Even though they were a few years behind the trends in England, prospering colonists began to adopt the styles of the world they had left behind. "The central-medallion style of . . . the late 18th century quilts . . . , so similar in appearance to English quilts of the same period, illustrates the strong European—and particularly English—influences on fashionable colonial taste."[22]

Even after the Revolutionary War, there was still some desire to emulate English fashions. It is no wonder, therefore, that strong interest in the bed and its adornments prevailed.

From 1650 to 1850 the bed was undoubtedly the single most important piece of furniture in the American household. For the affluent the elaborately carved high-post bed reigned supreme, and because of its expense "a fully dressed bed had no equal as a measure of a man's position."[23] Beds were magnificently outfitted, and a woman gave the greatest attention to the bed cover and other fittings.

In 1692 an inventory of the household belongings of Captain John Kidd, made shortly before he went to sea and turned pirate, listed various articles with which he and his wife Sarah began housekeeping, including:

"four bedsteads, with three suits of hangings, curtains, and valances to go with them. Feather beds, feather pillows, linen sheets, tablecloths, and napkins, ten blankets, and three quilts."[24]

In 1720 Miss Judith Sewall of a wealthy New England family, in preparation for her forthcoming marriage, ordered a list of articles from England:

[21]Alice Beer, *Trade Goods* (Washington, D.C.: Smithsonian Institution Press, 1970), pp. 35–36.

[22]Jonathan Holstein, *The Pieced Quilt* (Greenwich, Conn.: N.Y. Graphic Society, 1973), p. 30.

[23]Florence Montgomery, *Printed Textiles* (New York: Viking, 1970), p. 49.

[24]Marie Webster, *Quilts, Their Story and How to Make Them* (New York: Doubleday, Page & Co., 1915), pp. 70–71.

Blue Bedroom, Mt. Vernon, Virginia. The medallion quilt on this elaborate bed is patchwork and "broderie perse" appliqué. The colors are predominately red, blue and brown. The hand-netted fringe is 4⅛" deep. Virginia, mid-18th century. 99" x 110". (Courtesy of the Mount Vernon Ladies Association of the Union, Mt. Vernon, Virginia.)

"Broderie perse" appliqué quilt with tree of life design. The appliqué is cut out from glazed English chintz. Quilted in the border is "Sarah T. C. Miller 1830." The colors are off white, green, red, brown, blue and gold. 109" x 125". (Courtesy of the Shelburne Museum, Shelburne, Vermont.)

"A Duzen of good Black Walnut Chairs, A Duzen Cane Chairs, and a great chair for a chamber, all black Walnut. One Duzen large Pewter Plates, new fashion, a Duzen Ivory-hafted knives and forks. Four Duzen small glass salt cellars, Curtains and Vallens for a Bed with Counterpane, Head Cloth, and Tester made of good yellow watered camlet and trimming as may be enough to make cushions for the chamber chairs. A good fine larger Chintz quilt, well made."[25]

Further evidence of the importance of the bed and its furnishings during this period is found in the detailed description of the typical bed, found in the *Workwoman's Guide* for 1840:

"Bed furniture is composed of a top, a back, two head curtains, two foot curtains, one top outer and one top inner valance, one bottom valance, and sometimes extra drapery laid on the back of the bed. When beds are lined, the lining is put inside the curtains and within the top and back of the bed. . . . The curtains should just touch the ground, as also should the foot valance. . . . The valances accord with the rest, having often fringe added to give a greater finish."[26]

[25]Ibid., pp. 63–64.
[26]*Workwoman's Guide*, in Florence Montgomery, *Printed Textiles*, p. 63.

21

Floral appliqué quilt in "broderie perse" technique in the center. The appliqué is surrounded by printed and muslin borders. This quilt was in the trousseau of Mary Ann Barringer who married Dr. Charles Wilson Harris on July 1, 1828, at Poplar Creek, North Carolina. 97" x 97". (Courtesy of the Daughters of the American Revolution Museum, Washington D.C. Photograph by Gloria Allen and J. Young.)

With such great attention given to the bed, it is understandable that an equal amount of importance was placed on the quilts. Those in existence today that were made in the late 18th and early 19th centuries show, on the whole, finer workmanship and greater attention to detail than quilts made at any other time in our nation's history. In those early years, Americans looked to the styles in quiltmaking they had left behind in Europe and reproduced them in their new homeland. Thus, the medallion style and the "broderie perse" technique, popular in Europe, found their way into American quiltmaking.

Many exquisite examples of "broderie perse" medallion

Detail of quilt shown opposite. (Courtesy of the Daughters of the American Revolution Museum, Washington D.C. Photograph by Gloria Allen and J. Young.)

quilts can be found today in historic homes and museums along the Eastern seaboard. This technique seemed to be especially popular in the Southern colonies. Here, there was more time for amenities than in the North, where the struggle for survival was more intense. Furthermore, most of the settlers in the South were wealthy Englishmen who, upon their arrival, were able to establish large plantations with numerous slaves. They strove to achieve the height of elegance in their homes, their dress, and their furnishings—including their bedrooms. The Northern woman needed numerous quilts for warmth and had little time for detailed workmanship. The Southern woman, in a warmer climate,

Appliqué friendship quilt in the "broderie perse" technique made for Eliza Moore in New York and New Jersey, 1842–48. Each of the 72 smaller blocks is signed and dated and the larger center block says "Aunt Eliza Moore/Trenton, N.J./March 4, 1843." 101" x 104". (Courtesy of the Daughters of the American Revolution Museum, Washington D.C. Photograph by Gloria Allen and J. Young.)

needed fewer quilts, and, with her many slaves to do household chores, she had ample time to indulge in exquisite needlework. Furthermore, it is believed that the slaves did much of the fine needlework and quilting. The plantation owners were also better able to afford the latest goods, including fabrics from England and India. It is not surprising, therefore, that the South had a greater number of the early medallion quilts reminiscent of the Indian palampores.

Although the "broderie perse" technique was apparently an imitation of the Indian whole-cloth palampores, these early medallion quilts eventually took on a look all their own. One of the new adaptations was the medallion quilt with an eagle in the center. After the Revolutionary War and into the 19th century, this patriotic symbol appeared in numerous quilts, particularly during the 1820s with the cel-

Detail of friendship quilt opposite showing a closeup of the "broderie perse" appliqué. (Courtesy of the Daughters of the American Revolution Museum, Washington D.C. Photograph by Gloria Allen and J. Young.)

Detail of the center block of friendship quilt shown opposite. (Courtesy of the Daughters of the American Revolution Museum, Washington D.C. Photograph by Gloria Allen and J. Young.)

25

Eagle quilt, made in appliqué and reverse appliqué by Anna Catherine Hummell c. 1815. The eagle is made of a brown cotton print and done in reverse appliqué. The urn and floral motifs are appliquéd of roller-printed chintz in red and blue. The ivy border and 13 stars are also done in reverse appliqué. Frederick, Maryland 90″ x 92″. (Courtesy of the Daughters of the American Revolution Museum, Washington D.C. Photograph by Gloria Allen and J. Young.)

Detail of eagle quilt opposite showing reverse appliqué of eagle, stars and ivy border. (Courtesy of the Daughters of the American Revolution Museum, Washington D.C. Photograph by Gloria Allen and J. Young.)

ebration of 50 years of independence. Often the eagles were done in a reverse appliqué.

In some of the early examples of appliquéd chintz quilts, the central design was placed within a square that was turned diagonally "on point." As patchwork began to evolve, some of the medallions had a pieced block for the center motif rather than appliqué. Moreover, in addition to the printed and appliquéd borders, pieced borders were introduced, perhaps with an appliqué design for the center.

In contrast to the elaborate appliqué quilts of the 1700s, the pieced quilts of the same period were relatively simple. The quilt pictured on page 30 shows the typical large pieces of the early patchwork, and the one on page 33 shows the large pieced patchwork border, mixed with the reverse appliqué in both the central design and in some of the squares of the border. Another example of patchwork of the 18th century is seen on page 14, the *Penn Treaty* quilt made by Martha Washington. As the turn of the century approached, patchwork borders and designs gradually took on more sophistication.

Following the Revolutionary War, as Americans strove to establish their economic independence, textile printing began to develop. In the 1700s several calico printers established themselves in the New World. The most renowned of these was John Hewson, who came to America in 1773 and settled in Philadelphia. As a result of his participation in the American Revolution, the British put a price on his

Framed medallion comprised of cut-out chintz appliqué, pieced borders and floral striped borders. Colors are predominantly blue, brown and green. This quilt shows the transition from the "broderie perse" appliqué of the 18th century to the piecework of the 19th century. c. 1820. 109" x 118". (Courtesy of the Daughters of the American Revolution Museum, Washington D.C.

Detail of framed medallion quilt shown opposite. (Courtesy of the
Daughters of the American Revolution Museum, Washington D.C.)

Framed center quilt of the late 18th century with crewel embroidery of wool on a linen base. The patchwork is done with cotton and linen printed fabrics. The fringe is handmade of indigo blue dyed linen. The quilt belonged to the White family of Westminster, Mass. 90″ x 92″. (Courtesy of the Smithsonian Institution, Washington D.C.)

Medallion quilt top, c. 1860, pieced of tiny squares and rectangles, probably following a Berlin woolwork pattern and adapting it to patchwork. 100" x 102". (Author's collection.)

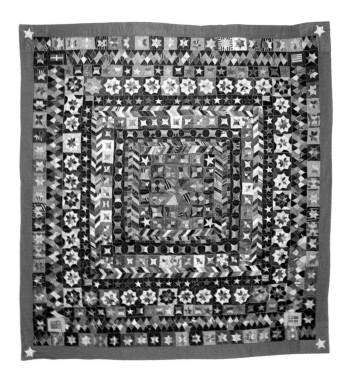

Central medallion quilt made of silks, c. 1880, Michigan. (Courtesy of Linda Reuther and Julie Silber, San Rafael, California.)

Pieced, appliquéd and embroidered wool quilt found in the estate of Mr. Graf who owned a bar and restaurant on the N.Y. waterfront and died in 1820. Along with the quilt was a note saying he had received it in payment from British sailors. Early 19th century. (Courtesy of the Smithsonian Institution, Washington D.C.)

Medallion quilt appliquéd of red and green cotton fabric on a white cotton background. Baltimore, mid-19th century. 90" x 94". (Courtesy of the Smithsonian Institution, Washington D.C.)

Appliquéd and pieced medallion quilt found in the attic of Pat McLaughlin's grandmother, Florence Alinda Furry Kennedy, who died in 1974 at the age of 96. When Mrs. Kennedy was living, Pat repeatedly asked her if there had been any quilts or quiltmakers in the family, and her reply always was, "No, we did not have to make quilts." This quilt was found after her death in the attic along with approximately 30 others. Because Mrs. Kennedy did not like quilts, nor make them herself, it is thought that the quilts were made by someone in her husband's family. Pennsylvania, c. 1850. 74" square. (Courtesy of Pat McLaughlin).

Amish Diamond quilt made of wool challis. Lancaster County, Pennsylvania, c. 1910-1920. 74" square. (Courtesy of Linda Reuther and Julie Silber, San Rafael, California).

Framed center quilt of reverse appliqué and patchwork. "M. Campbell" is embroidered in the center and "1795" is written in ink. New York. 91½" x 95½". (Courtesy of the Smithsonian Institution, Washington D.C.)

Detail of the pieced and appliquéd quilt made by M. Campbell in 1795. The entire central motif is worked in reverse appliqué. (Courtesy of the Smithsonian Institution, Washington D.C.)

Hand-printed coverlet by John Hewson printed in the style of an Indian palampore. The central design contains the familiar urn of flowers. Colors are brown, pink, red and blue on cream. Late 18th century. 103" x 105". (Courtesy of the Philadelphia Museum of Art, Philadelphia, Pennsylvania.)

head and destroyed much of his printing machinery, which he had most likely smuggled out of England. Hewson claimed to be the first calico printer in America, although there were others who also claimed that distinction.

Very little is known about any of the other printers and their textiles. However, a few excellent examples of Hewson's work are still in existence. One of the most famous of these, in the Philadelphia Museum of Art, is a beautiful "whole cloth" coverlet, hand printed in the style of an Indian palampore, which Hewson bequeathed to his daughter (See below). The urn of flowers, butterflies and exotic birds are familiar designs seen in the few pieces of Hewson's work that survive today.

Block-printed fabric by John Hewson showing the urn, flowers, birds and butterflies that Hewson is famous for. This was probably printed for the center of a quilt, imitating the "broderie perse" look. Early 19th century. (Courtesy of the Philadelphia Museum of Art, Philadelphia, Pennsylvania.)

Medallion quilt made by Zibia Smallwood Hewson, wife of John Hewson, from pieces printed by him. The colors are brown, yellow, red, blue, black, lavender and green. (The green was made by printing blue on yellow because it was not yet known how to produce a green dye. 103″ x 107″. (Courtesy of the Philadelphia Museum of Art, Philadelphia, Pennsylvania.)

Beginning of a quilt top made by or for Mary G. Jessop of Baltimore County, Maryland. The fabrics in the center are Hewson prints (c. 1800), but they have been cut apart from the traditional square that Hewson printed and then spread out and appliquéd onto a larger background. The corner motifs are appliqués of English glazed chintz of about 1830 and may have been added later. 65" square. (Courtesy of the Smithsonian Institution, Washington D.C.)

Square of fabric printed in imitation of "broderie perse" specifically for the center of a quilt. Second quarter of the 19th century. 27" square. (Courtesy of the Smithsonian Institution, Washington D.C.)

Along with John Hewson, other American and European printers began making cloth specifically for bed covers as well as yard-wide squares for the centers of quilts. These squares were substitutes for the earlier appliquéd chintz motifs. Gradually, and with this development, less time was spent on fine needlework. Fabrics were also printed specifically for border use. As Florence Montgomery states in *Printed Textiles*, "Among the fabrics of the 1790's suited to furnishing fabrics were luxuriant floral stripes. . . . Although probably printed in stripes . . . [they] were cut . . . for use as borders."[27]

By the 1800s, with textiles becoming available in Europe and the United States, the passion for authentic Indian cloth began to wane. However, the impact East Indian goods created on both European and American markets cannot be understated—the widespread use of cotton fabrics,

[27]Montgomery, p. 26.

Framed medallion quilt with central motif made from fabric printed specifically for quilts. Borders are cut from floral stripes. Second quarter of the 19th century. 75" x 77". (Courtesy of the Smithsonian Institution, Washington D.C.)

Star of Bethlehem quilt made by Mary (Betsy) Totten, of Tottenville, Staten Island, N.Y. This is one of at least two quilts Mary made with the same design. The roses and flowers are appliquéd of chintz; and the birds, vases, fruit and leaves are appliquéd of calico. The birds and chained-bud borders are worked in reverse appliqué. Early 19th century. (Courtesy of the Smithsonian Institution, Washington D.C.)

influences in color, pattern, and border use in fabrics, and our resulting medallion quilt design. The impact was indeed impressive.

"In the early 1600's the men who were to become the founders of the East India trading companies could not have realized what would happen when their ships landed with a new kind of cargo—painted cotton panels from India. . . . They had a great and lasting effect on 17th century world trade as well as on all subsequent printed fabric design."[28]

The *Star of Bethlehem* style quilt, very popular around 1800, seems to serve as a link between the beautiful appliquéd work of the 18th century and the pieced work of the 19th century. Numerous early examples of this type of quilt

[28]Florence Pettit, *America's Printed & Painted Fabrics 1600–1900* (New York: Hastings House, 1970), p. 54.

40

Piecework and appliqué **Star of Bethlehem** quilt made in the early 19th century. The star and borders are patchwork of early chintzes, English calicoes and copperplate prints. The square and triangles between the points of the star are done in beautiful cut-out chintz appliqué. (Courtesy of the Shelburne Museum, Shelburne, Vermont.)

survive, most of which have large center designs surrounded by borders. Many have elaborate appliquéd work in the squares and triangles between the points of the star and in the borders, thus indicating a desire to maintain the familiar appliqué techniques, while at the same time trying to attempt detailed piecework. The *Star of Bethlehem* has remained a popular design throughout our quilt history; but as the years went by, the complex borders and exotic treatment in the background were gradually discontinued.

The *Mosaic*, or *Honeycomb*, patchwork was another medallion style of the late 18th and early 19th centuries and was very popular in England. Most of these quilts were made in the technique we now call "English patchwork," where the fabric is basted over hexagonal-shaped pieces of paper and then the shapes are whip-stitched together. When complete, the paper is removed; although some of the old quilts still have the paper inside.

Star of Bethlehem with pieced center and borders. Early 19th century. The large squares and triangles are done of "broderie perse" type cut-out chintz appliqué. Jefferson County, Virginia. 98½" square. (Courtesy of the Daughters of the American Revolution Museum, Washington D.C.)

Honeycomb counterpane done in patchwork. The outer border is a copperplate print with exotic birds, flowers, fences and Chinese vases. The white areas are made of small hexagons. The quilt is said to have been made by Jane Morton Cook who was born in 1730 in Scituate, Massachusetts. The initials J^CM are cross-stitched on the linen back. (Courtesy of the Shelburne Museum, Shelburne, Vermont.)

Another type of medallion quilt popular at about the same time as the elaborately appliquéd spreads was the "white work" quilt. This was a whole-cloth quilt made almost exclusively of white cotton or linen or a cloth composed of both. The design element in the quilts came exclusively from the intricate quilting and stuffed work that embellished the entire top. Nearly all of these quilts were made in the central medallion style with elaborate centers often composed of such designs as eagles, flowers, trees, plumes, baskets or sunbursts. Corner motifs frequently echoed the elements in the center design and decorative borders surrounded the various sections. The background was completely quilted in an overall pattern—often of stippling. (See the last chapter, *Quilting,* for a description of stippling.) Florence Peto, in a 1948 article on white quilts for *Antiques Magazine,* stated that they "used the tree of life motifs or had a central medallion framed in a succession of borders or a central motif set in a field of scattered decoration finished with an important outer border."[29]

The design for the white quilts with their intricate borders and central motifs was probably also inspired by the Indian cloths that had a similar layout. Patsy and Myron Orlofsky in their book *Quilts in America* state: "The use of an important central design unit [in the all-white quilt] may be traced back through the eighteenth century to India."[30] Many of the quilts had ornate trees quilted in the middle very much like the tree of life designs on the palampores. Over the years the oriental look of the tree changed to resemble a weeping willow.

A truly outstanding example of a white work quilt was made by Virginia Ivey in 1856. Photographs of the whole quilt and a detail of one corner are shown on pages 46 and 47. Included as part of the stuffed work around the center circle just inside the fence is the following inscription: "1856 A Representation of the Fair Ground near Russelville, Kentucky." The quilt depicts the various things that impressed the maker at the fair. The center shows the exhibition tent. The judges inspecting items are visible on two levels. Around the tent is a parade of animals, horses drawing carriages and men on both foot and horseback. A fence circles the entire outer edge and within the fence are more horses and carriages and men. The detail is so fine that there are saddles on the horses, windows in the carriages and spokes on the wheels. Palm trees are pictured along with other varieties of trees not native to Kentucky, and one might assume that there was also a horticultural exhibit at the fair. There are approximately 150 stitches per square inch.

[29]Florence Peto, "Hand-made Elegance," *Antiques,* March, 1948.
[30]Patsy and Myron Orlofsky, *Quilts in America* (New York: McGraw-Hill, 1974), p. 199.

Stuffed white work. Detail of central motif of a quilt made by Orella Keeler Horton of Ridgefield, Connecticut, in the early 19th century. The borders are composed of diamonds, oak leaves, acorns, roses, cornucopias and grape leaves. There is a white cotton fringe on three sides. (Courtesy of the Daughters of the American Revolution Museum, Washington D.C.)

45

White work quilt made by Virginia Ivey in 1856 titled "A Representation of the Fair Ground near Russelville, Kentucky." Stuffed and corded work form the design, and the background is covered completely with stippling, 150 stitches per square inch. 94" x 94½". (Courtesy of the Smithsonian Institution, Washington D.C.)

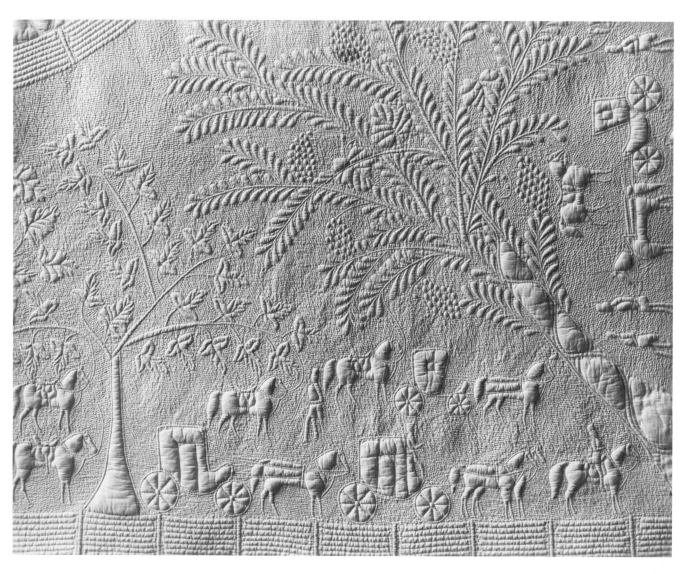

Detail of Fair Ground quilt, opposite. This area near one corner of the quilt shows a closeup of the elaborate stuffed and corded work and the stippled background.

Virginia Mason Ivey, maker of the Fair Ground quilt and numerous other fine quilts. She never married and was the daughter of Captain David Anderson Ivey and Mourning Mason.

Nine-patch medallion quilt, early 19th century, made from glazed chintz and cottons in brown, green and yellow. The muslin areas contain beautiful stuffed and corded work. 104″ square. (Courtesy of the Daughters of the American Revolution Museum, Washington D.C. Photograph by Gloria Allen and J. Young.)

Quite possibly, because of the difficulties involved in handling such a large piece of fabric, as in the early appliquéd and stuffed work quilts, women realized that it would be much easier to piece the quilt in units. More and more of the 19th century medallions are divided into parts consisting of various pieced, appliquéd and/or quilted borders surrounding the center. "The framed center quilt of the 1820s, 1830s, and 1840s is also characterized by a wide four-to-six-inch outside border, generally of floral chintz patterns."[31]

[31]Ibid. p. 300.

Detail of nine-patch medallion quilt opposite showing stuffed and corded work. (Courtesy of the Daughters of the American Revolution Museum, Washington D.C. Photograph by Gloria Allen and J. Young.)

By the mid 1800s medallion quiltmaking had given way almost entirely to the making of block-style quilts. Fabrics printed specifically for centers of quilts went out of fashion and, instead, cotton manufacturers printed imitation patchwork fabric to echo the block style of patchwork that by then had become so popular. Florence Montgomery in *Printed Textiles* states, "by the 1830's or 1840's geometric patchwork, without additions of embroidery, satisfied women's creative urge, and patchwork itself was simulated by printers."[32] Examples of medallion-style quilts are still

[32]Montgomery, p. 350.

found dating from the second half of the 19th century, particularly during the Centennial, when commemorative squares were used as centers. However, it is obvious that the block style, pieced quilt prevailed. Although there are some superb examples of medallion quilts from this time, they are few in number compared to those of the earlier period. Most of the medallion quilts from the period reveal neither the attention to detail nor the fine workmanship of earlier counterparts.

Pieced quilt top with *Mariner's Compass* and triangles. The colors are predominantly red, yellow, green and brown. Second quarter of the 19th century. 109″ square. (Courtesy of the Daughters of the American Revolution Museum, Washington D.C. Photograph by Gloria Allen and J. Young.)

Whig Rose, medallion quilt pieced and appliquéd of home-dyed fabric in turkey red, turkey yellow, green and pink. Hearts and flowers in the corners indicate it may have been a wedding quilt. c. 1840. 78″ x 79″. (From the collection of Al and Merry Silber, Birmingham, Michigan.)

Mary Jane Carr's Quilt is made in a variety of needlework techniques, including embroidery and appliqué. At the top of the spread, worked in brown cross-stitch, is "Mary Jane Carr's Quilt completed in 1854." Lancaster County Pennsylvania, 92″ x 99″. (Courtesy of the Shelburne Museum, Shelburne, Vermont.)

51

James K. Polk Quilt. Medallion style quilt made from patriotic fabrics depicting the 11th president of the United States and the American flag. The flags bear the textile maker's name. In the center of the quilt is a large brown and white printed fabric showing Polk with one star beside him; he favored the annexation of Texas. (Courtesy of the Shelburne Museum, Shelburne, Vermont.)

Civil War counterpane, pieced and appliquéd, made of chintzes, Scotch ginghams and paisley-patterned calicoes, many of which pre-date the Civil War period. Colors are brown, cream, blue, rose and dull red. This quilt was made by a wounded Union soldier during his convalescence. The female figure offering refreshments is copied from the trademark of a well-known chocolate. (Courtesy of the Shelburne Museum, Shelburne, Vermont.)

Pieced and appliquéd quilt signed on the back in India ink, "Rachel Vanderheyden No 4 1848". New York State, 84" square. (From the collection of Sandra Mitchell, Michigan.)

Pieced medallion quilt top in predominantly red, blue and grey with *Ohio Star* center. c. 1900. (Author's collection.)

Late in the 19th century, another type of medallion quilt emerged—the Pennsylvania Amish quilt with diamond-style centers. This style of Amish quilt, with its bold, graphic designs, is composed of a central square set on point within another square. Surrounding the squares are two borders, the inner narrow and the outer wider (see page 32). Although the origin of this style is unknown, there is speculation that it derived from the early framed medallion quilts.

Further interest in medallion quilts was negligible until the 1920s and 1930s, when a variation of the style began to develop. The medallion quilts of this period had larger central sections usually surrounded by only one border. The

Fig. 1. **Gorgeous Chrysanthemum Quilt** from early catalogue.

Home Arts Studio of Des Moines, Iowa, introduced a series of medallion quilt designs of this style. Patterns for the centers and borders were sold separately, so the maker could choose "her own" combination. One of the catalogues had a section on *New Designs in Medallion Center Quilts*, parts of which are interesting:

> "Here are beautiful designs in quilt patterns that lend themselves most effectively in bringing out the beauty of your own handiwork in the quilt that you make. The right medallion center, the quilting design and border cannot help but produce a quilt that will be the prize possession of your family for many generations. Each of the quilts illustrated on this page and the reverse page are available in Ready Stamped Quilt materials. This drastic revolution in the art of quilt making makes it possible for even a beginner to compete with experienced quilt makers. . . . The ready stamped quilt tops contain all the pieces that are necessary for making the complete top, corners and borders in their proper color arrangement."[33]

One of the designs shown in this pamphlet has been reproduced in fig. 1. The caption describing it reads:

> "Gorgeous Chrysanthemum Quilt—Pattern No. 383—Size 84x84 inches. The Gorgeous Chrysanthemum Quilt is just as beautiful as its name implies, when it is made up in any of the pastel colors. It is especially easy to piece and with ready stamped quilt patterns you can make it a masterpiece of your handiwork. Cutting guide for the patch work medallion center is P383. Special quilting design Q582 brings out the beauty of the quilting of the medallion center while quilting

[33]Home Arts Studio.

Indian Wreath, appliquéd multicolored quilt in violet, rose, red, green and yellow with princess feather quilting. Made by Charlotte Jane Whitehill in 1930. 90″ square. (Courtesy of the Denver Art Museum, Denver, Colorado.)

design Q438 is used for the corner. Patch work border B860 completes the quilt. Patterns are 10¢ each or should you desire all four patterns necessary to reproduce the quilt illustrated, order A383 price 35¢."[34]

Also of note during this period are the beautiful floral appliqué quilts made by some of the famous quiltmakers of the 1920s–1940s, such as Rose Kretzinger, Charlotte Jane Whitehill and Dr. Jeanette Throckmorton. What characterizes almost all of the medallion quilts of this period is a

[34] Ibid.

Appliquéd quilt made by Charlotte Jane Whitehill in 1930 from a pattern she borrowed from Mrs. S. J. Soden from Emporia, Kansas. The original pattern also had appliqué in the central portion. The quilt is multicolored in shades of rose, green, violet and reds. 92″ square. (Courtesy of the Denver Art Museum, Denver, Colorado.)

minimal use of borders, usually only an outer one, surrounding a very large central section.

Quiltmakers of the mid 20th century did very little to further medallion quilt design and seemed content to copy patterns or kits of styles that were developed in the 1930s and 1940s. It was not until the 1970s that the Bicentennial spawned a revival of interest. The medallion style seemed to offer unlimited possibilities for the creation of a quilt to express one's feelings about the American heritage. From the Bicentennial to the present, interest in medallion quilts has grown with more and more emphasis placed on workmanship, color, balance and style.

Orchid Wreath, appliquéd quilt made by Charlotte Jane Whitehill in 1933 from a pattern she acquired from Rose Kretsinger. The quilt is in shades of pink and violet. 92" square. (Courtesy of the Denver Art Museum, Denver, Colorado.)

Bicentennial Quilt made by Mary Granger. Begun in 1975 and finished in 1979. The quilt was started as a class project and grew. There are 13 stars within the swag border. 90″ square.

Bicentennial Quilt designed and made by Ellen Swanson, begun in August, 1974, and completed in September, 1977. Virginia, 74″ x 92½″.

Bicentennial Quilt designed by Hazel Carter who has a history of quilting in her family. Four generations of the maternal side of Hazel's family contributed blocks for the quilt. Virginia, 74½″ x 91½″.

Homecoming, pieced medallion quilt made by Yoko M. Sawanobori, May, 1978- February, 1979. Maryland, 82″ square.

Planning A Medallion Quilt

Structure

One wonders what has caused the dramatic surge of interest in medallion quilts in recent years. Perhaps it has something to do with the universal consciousness of balance and form that this type of quiltmaking can offer.

We are creatures of habit, and throughout our history we have structured our lives with order and balance. We generally sleep, eat, work and plan recreational activities at approximately the same times each day. Vacations usually occur about the same month every year.

Even though our lives are structured to a certain degree and are similar in pattern to the lives of many others, within that framework we are all individuals. We do not begin each week by preparing a schedule for every waking minute. To follow such a program would make life unbearably rigid and would stifle spontaneity. There would be no time to enjoy the beauty of a sunset, to watch a baby bird learning to fly, or to appreciate any of the hundreds of experiences that make our lives meaningful and unique.

Just as we appreciate some degree of order in our lives, many of us also prefer certain guidelines in our creative endeavors. I believe that being able to work within a structure is one of the reasons quiltmaking has become so popular. It offers an avenue for creativity in which people feel comfortable. The thought of a artist's blank canvas waiting to be filled is overwhelming to me, and I feel totally inept and unmotivated in that field. Although the guidelines of quiltmaking give me comfort, I feel it is important to remain open to spontaneous ideas and not to be unduly restricted by those same helpful guidelines.

The structure in a block-style quilt is based upon the fact that it is composed of a certain number of blocks. These can be set either squarely or diagonally, directly next to each other, or with alternate plain blocks or sashing. The quilt may or may not have a border. Yet within this basic outline thousands of quilts have been made, each with its own character and individuality. For a medallion quilt to be successful, it also needs a certain amount of structure.

However, the design is less tangible than a plan for the number and placement of blocks and a decision as to whether there will be a border.

Suzanne Offut, a friend who took one of my medallion workshops, wrote to me after the class and described the "mandala" concept. She thought that much of what I was teaching about the success of a medallion quilt was similar to this principle. She sent me the quotation below and said that she felt it also holds true for medallion quiltmaking.

> "Mandala is a circular design radiating out from a source or center. Used by all peoples of the earth and spontaneously appearing in nature, the mandala gives us a glimpse of the wholeness that lies beneath the veils of separation in our lives. The mandala created in different cultures as painting, stonework, embroidery . . . is a mirror of the natural order, it shows the organic and interdependent process of life."[35]

Interdependence is the key word. It is this order and interdependence that are so important for a successfully executed medallion quilt. Each part of the quilt must be related to another either through repeat of design elements, colors, fabrics or borders. It is these links that provide balance and order.

The key to medallion quiltmaking lies in the creation of a well-planned outline. I like to think of it in terms of a city. Some cities grow in a hodgepodge fashion with few building codes or restrictions. Before long a sprawling town has evolved with no charm but rather a conglomerate of sections unrelated to one another in either style or function. Conversely, a city whose future development was carefully mapped out years before the need for expansion arose maintains continuity as the growth occurs, because it is part of a plan. Changes can be made within that plan, but its existence creates a well-structured city as it grows. The same idea holds true in the making of a medallion quilt. If one merely builds from the center, arbitrarily adding borders according to whim, or attempts to execute as many different borders as possible, each part will look like what it is—an afterthought. No one part of the quilt should stand alone. If a careful outline is prepared with a theme to follow, the quilt can grow spontaneously. Yet the structure of the outline controls disorder and helps to produce a cohesive design.

Basic Outline

My basic philosophy about designing a medallion quilt, therefore, is somewhat contradictory. On the one hand, I do not believe the quilt should be totally planned with every detail graphed out before it is begun. On the other hand, I feel a central plan or outline is essential. If a medallion quilt is painstakingly designed on graph paper, one is less

[35]Illuminations, Inc., 1979.

Blue Star Sapphire, medallion quilt top made of American and French cottons by Jinny Beyer. Virginia, 1982. 88″ x 95″.

Right:

East Meets West, stenciled and pieced medallion quilt made by Barbara S. Bockman, June, 1981-May, 1982. The stenciled central motif is based on an ancient Japanese floral motif. 48″ x 68″.

Below:

Hungarian Peasant, pieced medallion quilt made by Kathryn Kuhn, 1979-1980. The quilt has a *Log Cabin* variation as the central medallion and in the borders. It owes its name to Kathryn's husband's Hungarian heritage. The quilt has a ''Hungarian feeling'' in both color and design, he says. 82″ x 98″.

Below right:

Scheherazade, pieced medallion quilt top made by Anne McClintic, May, 1980-May, 1982. 82″ x 106″.

Fig. 2.

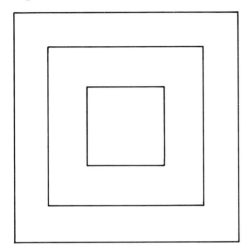

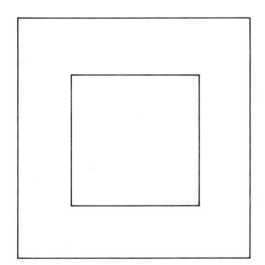

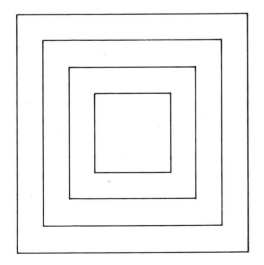

likely to be flexible and to make changes that should, perhaps, occur. The quilt could become rigid by duplicating in fabric what has been drawn on paper, without ever standing back to take a really good look and allowing the quilt to dictate changes as it grows. A design looks totally different on an 8″ x 10″ piece of paper than it does made into a full-size quilt. In addition, it is impossible to duplicate with colored pencils the effects of fabrics in the quilt. If a rough outline has been prepared, then changes can be made within that structure as the quilt grows.

It is difficult to form the outline concept of a medallion quilt in one's head. Basically it is comprised of major areas—the shape of the finished quilt, size and shape of the center, width of border areas, size and placement of units within major sections. The outline for a medallion quilt provides the structure to follow just as the number of blocks and the set provide the structure in a block-style quilt.

Do not expect to sit down and immediately draw an outline and have it be perfect. The entire process will take *time*. Begin by making some pencil sketches and getting a few ideas down on paper. Those sketches will help trigger other thoughts and before you know it, all the pieces will begin to fall into place.

Shape of the Quilt

The first step in creating an outline is to decide whether the quilt is going to be square or rectangular. Most quilters refer to a quilt that has two sides longer than the other as rectangular. Because a rectangle means having all right angles, it can also be square. However, for our purposes, we will refer to an elongated quilt as a rectangle and one in which all sides are equal as a square. Unless you are planning a wall quilt or a king-size quilt (which is usually square), chances are that you will want it rectangular. Whichever shape you choose is very important to the rest of the planning of the quilt, so it should be the first area to mark on the outline.

Major Parts of the Quilt

The second step in preparing the outline is to decide how many major areas the quilt will have. After working with medallion quilts for several years, I have found that certain concepts repeat themselves in terms of what seems to work and what does not. Many times these ideas suddenly crystallize, and I am able to verbalize them. Not long ago it became apparent to me that most of the successful medallion quilts I have seen have three major parts—a center section (this is not only the central motif but whatever makes up the entire central part of the quilt), the area between the central portion and the edge of the bed, and the outer border (this is usually the drop over the bed). In the three diagrams in fig. 2, the one with three divisions seems more balanced than the ones with two or four divisions.

Central Design

Before actually determining what shape the major areas of the quilt will take, one should decide about the center design. It is wise to have a fairly good idea about the central motif before planning the outline. The shape of the center can have a big influence on the overall outline of the quilt. It is important to note that the central motif should not take up the entire center section of the quilt. It is only one part, with borders and plain areas of fabrics combining with it to make up the entire central section.

The central motif in a medallion quilt is, of course, the focal point. As such, it should be something that is eye-catching, that will immediately bring your eye to the center, yet at the same time draw it out again so that it forms a link to the rest of the quilt. It should not be a contained unit. For example, as an all-over design the *Grandmother's Flower Garden* makes a beautiful quilt; yet an individual flowerette from that pattern would be inappropriate for the center of a medallion because it neither radiates nor acts as a focal point.

Any designs that give the illusion of reaching out or radiating—points stretching to the corners, stars, mariner's compasses, sunburst designs, etc.—are the kind to consider for the central motif. Best of all is to design your own radiating center, or take a traditional design and change it to suit the mood of your quilt. On pages 70 and 71 are a few examples to illustrate the types of designs that would and would not be effective as central motifs.

Center Section of the Quilt

Placement of the center design within the first major section of the quilt is a very important consideration. If it is set square and the remainder of the quilt also follows the square with border after border added around and around, it becomes monotonous (fig. 4). It is much more interesting to

Fig. 3. **Grandmother's Flower Garden**.

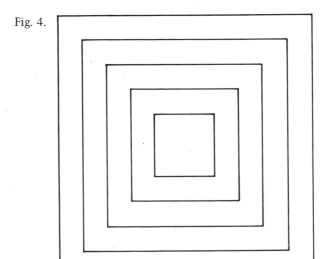

Fig. 4.

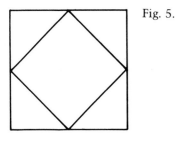

Fig. 5.

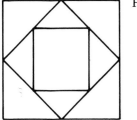

Fig. 6.

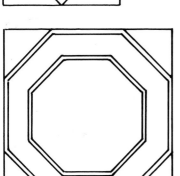

Fig. 7.

vary the placement of the design elements in the quilt. For example, it is possible to begin with a square set on point and then place that into a square, as Yoko Sawanobori has done in her quilt shown on page 62, or as in fig. 5. Some of the quilts illustrated in the photographs have begun in this same way. You may want to glance through and see how different each quilt looks even though the central placement on many of them is similar. The elements beyond the center—design, color, borders, shape of other sections—all contribute to make each quilt unique.

Another possibility is to start with a square, set that into a square set on point, and then square it off again (fig. 6).

Every quilt does not have to begin with a square. If the center design is composed of the elements of an eight-pointed star or another suitable design, you might want to begin with an octagon shape and build on that before squaring it off (fig. 7). Look at Betty Larson's quilt on page 84 or Boots Bartell's , on page 86.

Many people begin with a circular design for their central motif. Why be in a rush to square it off? Try building on the circle before finally putting it into a square. (Fig. 8).

Fig. 8.

Some designs that would be effective as central motifs:

*Fig. 9. **Safe Harbour** (36-square, nine- patch category). Designed by Jinny Beyer for the 1982 Sea Pines Seminar.

Fig. 10. **Mariner's Wheel** (curved design, 16 divisions category). Designed by Jinny Beyer for the 1981 Sea Pines Seminar.

Fig. 11. **Compass Rose** (curved design, 32 divisions category). Designed by Jinny Beyer for the 1981 Sea Pines Seminar.

Fig. 12. **Castle Wall** (eight-pointed star category). *Godey's Lady's Book*, 1851.

Fig. 13. **Dutch Rose** (eight-pointed star category). *Hearth and Home*, 1870.

Fig. 14. **Star of North Carolina** (eight-pointed star category). *Ladies' Art Company*, 1922.

*The designs in this book have been labeled according to the categories developed in my previous two books. The plastic grid from *The Quilter's Album of Blocks and Borders* can be used to help understand how to draft these designs.

Some designs that would *not* be effective as central motifs:

Fig. 15. **Magic Circle** (64-square, four-patch category). *Ladies' Art Company,* 1898.

Fig. 16. **Tall Pine Tree** (five-patch category). *The Romance of the Patchwork Quilt in America,* 1935.

Fig. 17. **Coxey's Camp** (64-square, four-patch category). *Ladies' Art Company,* 1898.

Fig. 18. **Squares and Stripes** (64-square, four-patch category). *Ladies' Art Company,* 1898.

Fig. 19. **Swastika Patch** (nine-patch category). *Ladies' Art Company,* 1928.

Fig. 20. **Pineapple**. *Ladies' Art Company,* 1898.

Joan Christensen and Mary Albright have both added pieced borders around their center circles before setting them in a square. Joan's quilt is shown on page 156 and the center of Mary's quilt is shown below.

When the circle eventually is placed in a square, the major consideration is how large the circle should be in relation to the square. My own feeling is that it should almost fill the space, with the sides of the circle nearly touching the edges of the square, with not more than half an inch from the edge of the circle to the sides of the square. Look at the two diagrams in fig. 21. In the one with the smaller circle, there is too much space at the corners and the circle appears to be floating. The second diagram shows the circle almost filling the space, which appears more balanced. Thus the eye will tend to project the design beyond the square so it will form a link to the rest of the quilt. The same holds

The Journey, central motif of pieced medallion quilt made by Mary Albright, 1980-1982. The name for the quilt comes from the fact that Mary commuted six hours each way to the class in which she planned the quilt. North Carolina, 120" square.

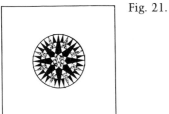

Fig. 21.

true with any design, whether it is in a square, diamond, oval or rectangle—a lot of background space will isolate the center design. Interdependence is the key, and if one part appears to be floating, there is no connection between that and the rest of the quilt. If the points or parts of the design almost touch the edge, they appear to be reaching beyond it, linking themselves to the next part of the quilt.

Frequently I am asked how large the center design should be. There are no hard and fast rules, and I do not like to give formulas because the possibilities are endless. The best guide is a feeling you get from studying sketches that show how the various parts relate to each other proportionately. Suffice it to say that a ten-inch design centered in a king-size quilt would appear insignificant, and a 20-inch central motif on a crib quilt would be overwhelming. I do feel, however, that when considering the entire central *section* of the quilt (the first major division that includes the center motif), there does seem to be a general proportion that works. If you take the entire area of the first two major sections of the quilt (this is usually the part that will fit on top of the bed) and divide it into quarters, an area slightly larger than one of those quarter sections will generally be a good size for the central part of the quilt. (See fig. 22.) Do not confuse this with the center *design*. The central part consists of the center design plus any borders or other elements that make up the entire first section of the quilt. Fig. 23 shows a possible outline with the first section complete.

Fig. 22.

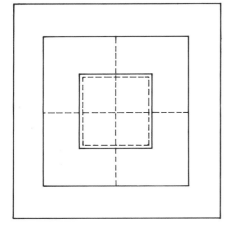

Fig. 23.

Elongating the Quilt

Up to this point the illustrations and discussions have dealt with square designs that are obviously easier to make in a medallion style. Because square bedcovers are usually only used on king-size beds, most medallions need to be elongated into rectangles. Having studied medallion quilts in general and those made by my students in particular, I have come to the conclusion that the design is usually more effective if the elongation occurs within the first major section of the quilt and as close to the center as possible. Then when that part of the quilt is finished it will already be in a rectangle; from that point on, all areas added will be of equal widths. It is more pleasing to look at a design in which all major sections are in proportion to each other rather than one that has some parts out of sync. You can see in the designs in fig. 24 how the proportions of the quilt differ depending upon where the elongation occurs, and how much more balanced the quilt looks with the elongation in the central section.

No matter where the quilt is elongated or what method is used, it must appear as a well-planned, well-balanced entity. It must look as though it is an integral part of the design, not an afterthought that was tacked on because the quilt *had* to be longer. Obviously, surrounding a square with border after border and then suddenly adding something at the top and bottom to form a rectangle is not going to look integrated.

Fig. 24.

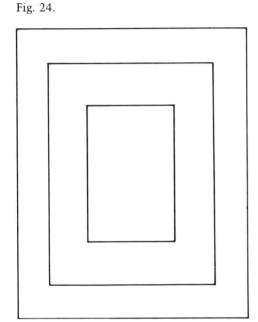

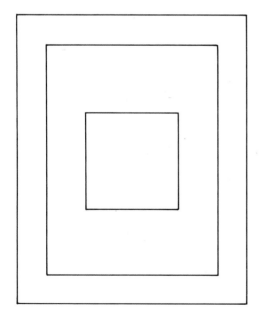

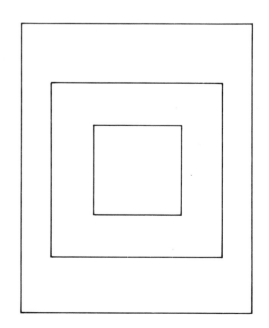

There are numerous ways to make a quilt longer and still maintain the look and harmony of a well-planned design. A few suggestions will be offered here, and they should serve to create new ideas that will make your medallion quilt unique.

One of the easiest and most obvious ways to elongate a quilt is to begin with a rectangular design. This is not as difficult as it sounds. First decide how much longer the entire quilt is to be than its width. If you want the length of the finished quilt to be 10″ longer, then plan the center design to be 10″ longer than its width (12″ x 22″ or 15″ x 25″, etc.). Almost any of the traditional patchwork designs can be redrafted to fit within a rectangle. For example, a 16-square, four-patch design such as *Centennial* (fig. 25) is usually drafted by dividing whatever size block you need into 16 equal squares. This is done by either folding or ruling off four equal divisions on each side of the square. The design is then drafted within the grid created. To draft the same design into a rectangle, each side is still divided into fourths; only the divisions along the length of the rectangle will be greater than those along the width. The same will hold true with designs based on nine-patch, five-patch or seven-patch grids. (See figs. 26, 27 and 28.) Virginia Suzuki began with a rectangular design in the center of her quilt *Omaki* shown on page 155.

Fig. 25. **Centennial** (16-square, four-patch design). *Ladies' Art Company*, 1898.

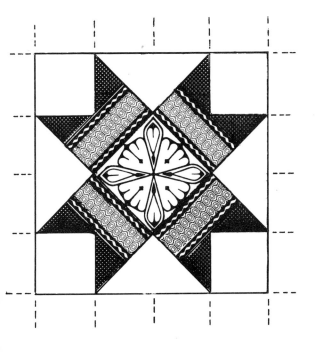

Fig. 26. **California Sunset** (36-square, nine-patch category). Designed by Jinny Beyer, 1979.

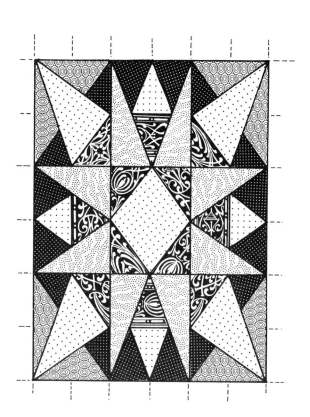

Fig. 27. **Providence Quilt Block** (five-patch category). *Ladies' Art Company*, 1898.

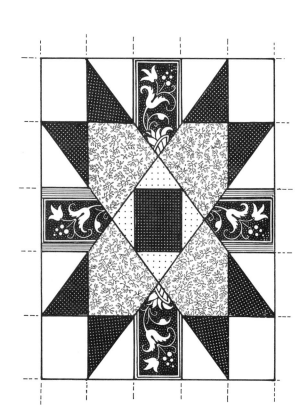

Fig. 28. **Our Country** (seven-patch category).
Kansas City Star, 1939.

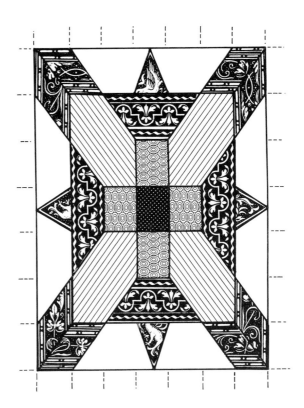

The central motif does not necessarily have to be rectangular in order for the first section to end up as a rectangle. A design could be drafted into the shape of a diamond and that could be placed inside a rectangle as in Pat Mc-Laughlin's quilt on page 106. (See fig. 29). It is also possible to take one of the sunburst or mariner's compass designs, draft it into an oval (see *Patchwork Patterns* pages 172-173 for instructions on how to draft an oval, and designs to fit inside) and then fit that into a rectangle, as Carolyn Lynch has done in her quilt on page 78. (See fig. 30). If you like the idea of an octagon in the center of your quilt, an elongated octagon is another possibility. (Fig. 31).

Fig. 29.

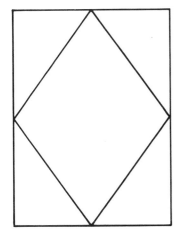

Fig. 30.

Fig. 31.

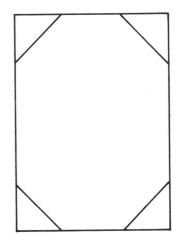

Oval Medallion, pieced medallion quilt made by Carolyn Lynch, 1980. The design allows an area to be tucked under the pillow. Virginia, 72″ x 92″.

Fig. 32. **Swamp Patch** (nine-patch category). *Godey's Lady's Book,* 1858.

The distortion of a design caused by stretching it to fit into an oval, rectangle or diamond may seem unappealing. If that is the case, instead of drafting the whole design into a rectangle look for ways in which you could maintain the center as square but stretch parts of the design outside the square. The *Swamp Patch* design, fig. 32, is an example. Follow figs. 32a-d to see how it has been elongated. The result of the modification barely resembles the original *Swamp Patch.*

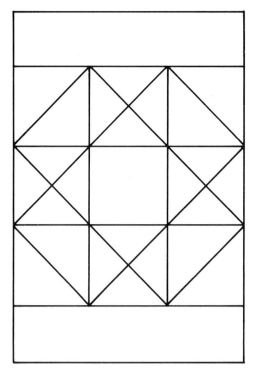

Fig. 32a. Decide how much longer the quilt needs to be; if it is 12″, add 6″ to the top and bottom of the design.

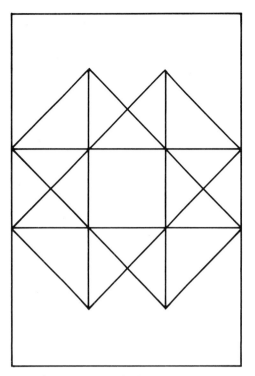

Fig.32b. Now erase the lines forming the top and bottom of the square.

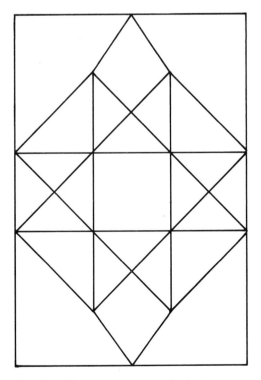

Fig. 32c. The next step is to look for ways to connect the open lines with the upper edges of the rectangle. Usually some kind of points are very effective because they will radiate outward to other parts of the quilt. Therefore you might extend one larger point in the *Swamp Patch* block to the top and bottom edges of the rectangle.

Fig. 32d. At this point the design looks somewhat awkward so I would add shorter points at the sides of the block and have them overlap a border so as not to increase the width of the design.

Using this technique, it is possible to create any number of original designs from traditional patterns. To experiment, find a book with many quilt block illustrations. On a piece of tracing paper, make a series of rectangles. The width of the rectangles should be the same as those of the designs in the book. Then place the rectangle over the patterns you like and figure out ways to elongate them. The following pages contain a few more examples.

Fig. 33. **Swallowtails** (64-square, four-patch category). Designed by Jinny Beyer for the 1982 Sea Pines Seminar.

Fig. 34. **Atlantic Star** (five-patch category). Designed by Jinny Beyer for 1982 Sea Pines Seminar.

Fig. 35. **Rolling Compass** (curved design, 16-divisions category). Designed by Jinny Beyer for the 1982 Sea Pines Seminar.

Sometimes a more interesting elongation can occur if the design is placed diagonally first, as shown in *Dahlia*. (Fig. 36).

Fig. 36. **Dahlia** (eight pointed star category). Designed by Jinny Beyer, 1982.

81

Figs. 37, 38 and 39 show two versions of the same design—one where the design began set square and the other set diagonally. This technique was used to create the center motif of my medallion quilt, *Blue Star Sapphire* on page 65. I used a design based on an eight-pointed star and elongated it by bringing points out beyond the design, using an odd shape instead of a rectangle. Katherine Kuhn has also used the same idea in her quilt *Robin's Star* shown on page 104. Try experimenting with other designs using this approach.

Fig. 37. **Carolina Pinwheel** (36-square, nine-patch category). Designed by Jinny Beyer for the 1982 Sea Pines Seminar.

Star of Persia, pieced medallion quilt made by Kathryn Kuhn, summer, 1978-March, 1979. The design was inspired by a handmade mosaic box from Persia. 84″ x 96″.

Beyer Patch, pieced medallion quilt made by Marilyn Titman, February, 1978-February, 1980. The central motif is the traditional *Potomac's Pride* block, and the borders and area surrounding the center are Marilyn's original design. 84″ x 98″.

Mountain Aster, pieced medallion quilt made by Louise Hayes, 1978-1980. The central motif is an adaptation of an old quilt pattern, *Fringed Aster*. The border triangles were inspired by *Delectable Mountains*. 84″ x 100″.

By the Golden Gate, pieced medallion quilt made by Virginia Suzuki, April, 1981-April, 1982. The design is based on a hexagon. 90″ x 100″.

Tulip Garden, pieced and appliquéd medallion quilt top made by Betty Larson, Feburary, 1980-November, 1981. 96″ square.

Eclipse, pieced medallion quilt made by Judy Spahn, February, 1978-May, 1979. The design is a mosaic made up of two-inch equilateral triangles. 80½" x 86½".

Tripoli, pieced medallion quilt top made by Audrey Waite, February, 1980-February, 1982. The design inspiration came from an ivory-inlaid chessboard Audrey's husband purchased while on a trip to Tripoli, Libya. 85" x 95".

Star Variable, pieced medallion quilt top made by Ellen Swanson, completed in January, 1982. 87″ x 103″.

Stars and Chains, pieced medallion quilt made by Boots Bartell, February, 1978-April, 1981. The design was inspired by a small quilt made in 1850 pictured in the *Folk Quilts Calendar, 1978.* 78″ x 94″.

Medallion #10, pieced medallion quilt top made by Patricia B. Madlener, 1978. 92″ x 104″.

New York Beauty, pieced medallion quilt made by Colleen Gosling, 1978-1982. The central design was inspired by the traditional *New York Beauty* design. 83″ square.

Fig. 38. **Eastern Sunrise** (64-square, four-patch category). Designed by Jinny Beyer for the 1982 Sea Pines Seminar.

Fig. 39. **Sea Crystal** (eight-pointed star category). Designed by Jinny Beyer for the 1982 Sea Pines Seminar.

Persian Carpet, pieced medallion wall quilt made by Linda Hause, March, 1979-April, 1982. Maryland, 46½" x 51½".

If you still want to begin with a square design but want to fit it into a rectangle as soon as possible, there are other ways it can be done. One is to put the square on point and fit it into a rectangle. In fig. 40 the border on the rectangle is 5″ wide. The square just touches the border at the top and bottom but cuts through it on the sides. In this way 10″ have been added to the length of the quilt. Another possibility is to fit the square into a diamond. (Fig. 41).

If the central motif of the quilt is based on a hexagonal design, the problem is simplified. The hexagon is already slightly elongated and will fit within a rectangle. This may not give quite as much length as is needed; but if it does, it is a relatively easy solution to the elongation problem. (Figs. 42 and 43). *Suzi's Box* (page 120), *Eclipse* (page 85) by Judy Spann, *Star of Persia* (page 83) by Katherine Kuhn and *Persian Carpet* (page 89) by Linda Hause were all designed using a hexagonal design as the central motif.

There are many possibilities for lengthening a quilt. Ellen Swanson's *Star Variable* (page 86), Ann McClintic's *Scheherazade* (page 66), Katherine Kuhn's *Hungarian Peasant* (page 66) and Louise Hayes' *Mountain Aster* (page 83) all have still different solutions for elongation, and there are

Fig. 40.

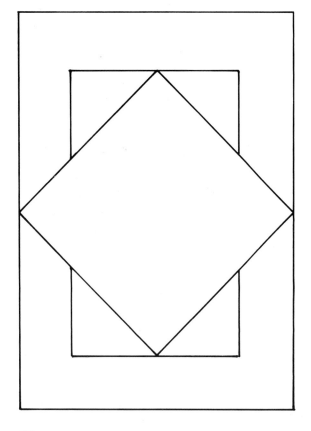

Fig. 41.

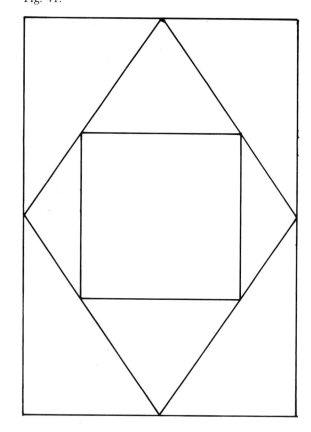

Fig. 42. **Asteroid** (hexagon category). Designed by Jinny Beyer, 1979.

Fig. 43. **Savannah Beautiful Star** (hexagon category). *Ladies' Art Company*, 1972.

many more ways that it can be done successfully. The most important thing to remember is that if the elongation is not incorporated smoothly into the quilt design in the basic outline stage, there may be problems later. You cannot go merrily building around a square and when half finished try to figure out how to elongate it and have it look as though it was planned from the start. The farther out the elongation is begun, the greater the chance of upsetting the balance of the design.

Betty Larson had trouble with her beautiful appliqué and pieced quilt shown on page 84. Unsure about how to lengthen the quilt, she continued building around the octagon; and when she finally started trying to figure out how to elongate it, nothing worked. Anything she tried seemed to spoil the overall effect. She became so frustrated that she put it away for almost a year. One day she came to my house for a class and brought her quilt. We all offered suggestions but still nothing seemed to work, and she went away more discouraged than ever. Then about a week later she called, bubbling with excitement. She said, "A miracle happened! I have the rest of my quilt all worked out. I'm so excited!" I asked her what happened and she replied, "I had the most incredible experience—my quilt spoke to me." "Spoke to you?" I asked in amazement. "Yes," she said. "I laid it down on the floor and was trying once again to figure out what I could do to make it longer and all of a sudden my quilt looked up at me and spoke." "What did it say?" I asked. Betty said, "It just looked up and in a big, deep, booming voice said 'I want to be square!'"

For the first time she realized that she could go ahead and finish it as a square quilt, that she had worked too far from the center based on a square to change, and to alter it would spoil the continuity. By retaining the square shape, all the design elements would continue in balance and the symmetry she started with would not be interrupted.

Pillow Tuck

Something you may want to include in your quilt is an area to tuck under the pillow. If a medallion quilt has been designed to be symmetrical from the center, obviously the design will be broken up when a part of the quilt disappears under the pillows. If your main concern is to have the quilt look completely balanced when it is on the bed, then you should do one of two things. Either plan to add an extra border, piece of fabric, etc. somewhere in the outline to allow for the pillow tuck, or make pillow shams and do not put the quilt over the pillows. Carolyn Lynch wanted her quilt (on page 78) to look perfectly symmetrical on a bed, so she added an extra section at the top to allow for the pillow tuck. For the most part, I do not think the area tucked under the pillow takes away from the overall look when the quilt is on the bed; however, if it is something you wish to consider, it should be planned in the initial outline stage.

Completing the Outline

Once you have decided what shape the quilt will be, how many main areas it will have, and have a fairly good idea about the central motif and its placement within the center section of the quilt, the outline is well on its way. It is at this point that you should redraw the outline with a general idea of the measurements of the quilt, the size of the center and the width of the various border areas. It is important, however, to remain flexible. You may get to the edge of the quilt and discover that if that last border is added it will be too much. On the other hand, you may be finished according to your sketch and discover that the only way the quilt will truly be complete is to add one final border or fabric strip.

Fig. 44. To make your outline, mark the outer dimensions of the quilt on a piece of graph paper. Next, mark the area for the outer border (which is most likely the drop over the edge of the bed), and finally put the center section in the middle of the outline. At this point study the proportions of your drawing. If the various parts do not seem balanced, then try again until the proportions look right. Your outline should resemble this one. Of course, the center section on your quilt and its overall shape probably differ from the one illustrated.

Fig. 45a-c. Next, fill in the area between the first and last sections. Once again, don't be concerned with exact design but rather general placement. This area can be broken up with square blocks, square blocks placed on point, triangles repre-

Fig. 44.

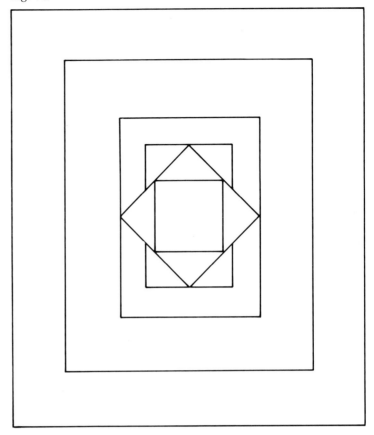

Fig. 45a.

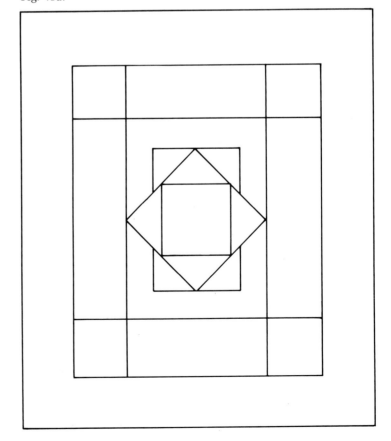

senting half squares, diamonds, plain fabric with blocks at the corners, etc. The main consideration is to give the outline some variety so that it is not merely a series of borders going around and around and around. These examples all have used the same center section as fig. 44, opposite, but varying the next section can totally change the look of the quilt. It may be necessary to make some adjustments in the size of the sections in order to fit in the various shapes. In the case of fig. 45b, once the diagonally set squares were placed in the second section, the outline seemed also to need a diagonally set square placed in the very center of the quilt. Decisions must be made as you go along adding new parts as the need arises. That is why it is so important to remain flexible.

Fig. 45b.

Fig. 45c.

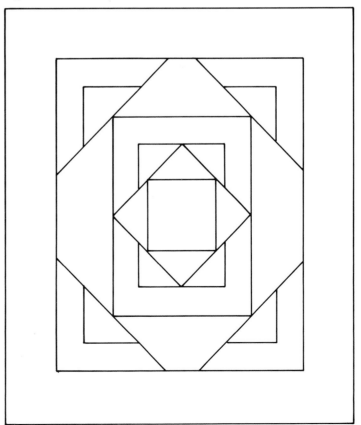

Fig. 46 a-c. As you are creating the basic outline, look for places where smaller printed or plain fabric borders, or patch-work, appliqué or quilted borders might be used. Those areas can be added to the outline as you are working on it. Sometimes it is necessary to fill in a few extra inches, and a border could effectively solve such a problem. These examples are the same as those in fig. 45 except for the addition of areas for smaller borders.

Fig. 46a.

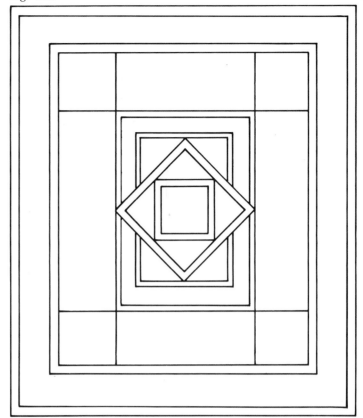

Fig. 46b.

Fig. 47. This is the outline I used for my *Ray of Light* medallion quilt shown on page 157. Notice the white triangles with the sawtooth piecing on the outer border of this quilt. One of my main considerations was to have the triangles on the outside directly opposite the same triangles on the inside. The whole effect would have been ruined if this had not occurred or had the triangles in one border not been the same size as those in the other. In order for the corners to turn uniformly, and for the triangles to remain opposite each other, the width of the border in between the triangles (the area marked A) was crucial. That border either had to be half the width of the base of the triangle (B), or the entire width in order for the triangles to meet at the corners. It would have been too wide if it were the entire width, so I chose half. I cannot overstress the importance of thinking through the sizing of squares or triangles that you want to meet opposite one another.

The measurement across the base of the triangle (B) was the determining factor in the measurements of the entire quilt. That width was the same as the diagonal dimension across the squares in the second section of the quilt (C). In order for those squares to go around evenly, I planned the width of the central section (D) to be the equivalent of four of those triangles—three triangles centered with a half triangle on each corner. The base of each triangle ended up measuring 10″. That meant that the central section had to be 40″ square and the width of border A had to be half the width of the 10″ triangle—or 5″. I knew I wanted the radiating compass in the center of the quilt, but was not yet sure which designs or fabrics I was going to use in the other sections. Those decisions were made as I worked from the center outward. Elongation of the quilt came in the second section when I added an extra triangle at the top and bottom.

Fig. 47.

84×94

95

Maintaining Continuity

Once the outline for the quilt has been worked out, it is best to start with the central motif and allow the quilt to grow from there. Each addition of fabric and design will help to dictate what should come next. It is here that the interdependence of each part is *so* crucial. The most important aspect of the entire quilt is to maintain its continuity, so that each part is related to some other part. If the continuity is not there, the parts will not be integrated and the quilt will lack balance and symmetry.

There are three important ways to maintain continuity in a quilt—through repetition of design elements, borders and fabrics. Each of these is of equal importance to the overall plan of a quilt.

First of all, I feel that no one design element should stand alone. Look for ways to use the shapes found in the central motif when planning the border designs in the rest of the quilt. Try not to introduce any totally new shape or design element after the first major section. If the center design has curves, repeat the curves somewhere else. Do not plan an appliqué center surrounded entirely by geometric patchwork designs with no further use of appliqué. There is nothing wrong with mixing patchwork and appliqué, however, they should be alternated so that one element does not appear as an unrelated afterthought. (Betty Larson's quilt, *Tulip Garden* on page 84, is an excellent example of how the two can work compatibly.) See the difference in the two designs in fig. 48. The one in which the appliqué and patchwork have been integrated has much more continuity than the one with appliqué only in the center.

The same holds true with border designs. It is so much more effective to use a border design at least twice or to echo something that has been used before than to keep adding new borders.

Repetitive use of fabrics also helps to add continuity to the quilt. Try to use all the fabrics in the first major section. Then use each of them at least once more in some other part. It is the same with striped fabrics that may be cut for borders. Plan to have enough yardage so that each fabric border can be used at least twice in the quilt. (More on the use of border designs and fabrics can be found in the chapters beginning on pages 99 and 121.)

A medallion quilt can be very busy. Therefore, one important consideration in the overall outline is to leave some areas free of design. Do not feel that you have to put patchwork or appliqué throughout every single inch. In fact, the eye *needs* some resting places between various design elements. This is best achieved by using a large print or plain fabric in areas between some of the designs of the quilt. In addition, use restraint in the number of fabrics and designs you choose. The more design elements and different borders and fabrics that are employed, the busier the quilt is apt to be. Use the medallion quilt not as a sounding board for all of the designs that you had someday hoped to try, but rather as an exercise in restraint. No fabric, border or design element should stand alone. It should be repeated in part or at least echoed somewhere else in the quilt. Careful planning of such interdependence is what gives the quilt its balance and memorable effect.

Fig. 48a.

Fig.48b.

Star Surrounded, pieced medallion quilt made by Ellie Bennett, March, 1979-January, 1981. Pennsylvania, 70″ square.

Fabric

The use of colors and fabrics in medallion quilts is a purely subjective matter and depends on the individual quiltmaker and the mood she wants to convey. In fact, I do not like to make any specific color recommendations. Because the possibilities are endless, the choice should be entirely one's own. I feel that value and light and dark contrasts are the most important considerations. In my book, *The Quilter's Album of Blocks and Borders*, I described in detail my own ideas regarding fabric use. In this text I will give general thoughts to consider no matter what types of fabrics or colors are used.

Everyone is familiar with the age-old question: Which came first, the chicken or the egg? The counterpart of that question throughout the history of quiltmaking has been: Should one select fabrics and design a quilt around them, or design a quilt and then select fabrics to suit the design? Though I would not presume to enter the debate over chicken and egg, I would venture to say with regard to quilting that both approaches are valid, but a combination of the two is ideal. In many instances fabrics will inspire a design; in others, a design will dictate the fabrics. My *Blue Star Sapphire* quilt on page 65 was planned around a beautiful printed border, and the fabrics were chosen long before I ever designed the quilt. When the center was pieced and "the" border was ready to be added, I was dismayed with the result. It just did not work. Not only was it necessary to find another border, but many of the original fabrics in the center also had to be replaced. So much for preplanning!

Patience is an absolute must both to the designing and making of a medallion quilt. Do not try to determine in advance exactly which fabrics are to be used in various areas. Until something is pieced, it is impossible to know how it is going to look. Concentrate on the center and work out from it. When the central design is satisfactory, lay it next to other colors and fabrics to determine what combination will enhance the center most effectively. Be flexible! Realize that you may sew something together that does not work out, and be prepared to replace some pieces if you are not satisfied.

Types of Fabrics

My approach to quiltmaking is basically traditional. This is particularly true of my desire to use only 100% cotton fabrics in my quilts. I use a variety of other fabrics in quilted garments, wall hangings and small projects; but these are all items that are not expected to have the durability of quilts. All-cotton fabrics are preferable for quilts for several reasons.

First, cotton has a softer look than fabrics blended of cotton and polyester. The very nature of polyester causes it to be somewhat rigid and crease-resistant. Therefore, when used in a quilt, the areas not held down by quilting puff up artificially and do not look soft. It also seems easier to push a needle through fabrics of all cotton than those with a blend of fibers.

Usually a seam allowance of one-quarter inch is used in quiltmaking. I have found that poly-cotton blend fabrics tend to ravel more easily than those of all cotton. Thus, seams in the blended fabrics are more likely to pull apart.

Quilting seems to look better on quilts made of all-cotton fabrics. The stitches and fabrics meld together and appear to become one. However, quilting stitches in polyester fabrics seem to lay on top of the fabric, never becoming a part of it; and any uneven stitches are much more noticeable.

With the introduction of polyester batting in recent years, quiltmakers have been confronted with the problem of "bearding." Manufacturers call this "fiber migration" and it occurs when polyester fibers in the batting work themselves through the weave of the fabric. The result is the appearance of a white fuzz on the surface of the quilt. The problem, of course, is more noticeable on dark fabrics. Bearding is much worse in fabrics made of artificial fibers than it is in those made of 100% cotton fabrics. Polyester blends seem to act as a magnet, drawing fibers from the batting up through the fabric. Some bearding will always occur when polyester batting is used, but it will not be as great with all-cotton fabrics. For less bearding the alternative is cotton batting, or a cotton-polyester blend batting with a low percentage of polyester fibers.

Prints vs. Solids

Whether prints, solids or a combination of both are used in a quilt is strictly a matter of personal preference. Solids tend to give a bolder, more graphic and contemporary look, prints a softer and, depending on the colors, often a more antique look.

In using prints, certain factors are helpful to keep in mind. For a variety in texture, have a contrast in the size of the prints. Use of all tiny prints can be monotonous just as the use of all large prints can be very busy. When purchasing fabrics, I try to avoid small prints with more than two colors, as I find they are difficult to combine effectively with other prints. I purchase multicolored prints only if they are of a large scale or in stripes suitable for borders. Fabrics with a sharp contrast between light and dark also mix less successfully than those with a more subtle blend between the colors.

Border prints are a favorite of mine and I am always on the lookout for them. Referred to as "repeat stripes" by the manufacturers, these are actually decoratively striped fabrics from which a stripe, or series of stripes, may be cut for use as borders in a quilt. Often a strip of fabric is needed to separate different areas within a quilt—especially a medallion quilt—and for this purpose border-print fabrics add a unique touch. (More on the use of border-print fabrics can be found in *Planning and Executing Borders*, beginning on page 121.)

Contrast

One of the most important considerations by far is that of the contrasts between light- and dark-colored fabrics; and unless a quilt is to be very subtle this is a major factor in its success. For example, the central motif of the quilt is the focal point and, as such, should initially capture one's attention. To do that it must be not only visible, but preferably striking. Study the design and decide which element should predominate. Whatever your choice, it should be composed of the darkest fabric set in the lightest background, or vice versa. If there is something special you want to use but it does not provide enough contrast to the adjoining fabric, try outlining the area between the two with a small, dark strip of plain fabric or a dark, narrow striped fabric. This technique can be extremely helpful when extra contrast is needed, and it also adds another dimension to the overall look of the quilt. (See *Planning and Executing Borders*, page 121, for more on the use of outline borders.)

Repeated Use of Fabrics

One important way to maintain continuity throughout a medallion quilt is by the repeated use of fabrics within the various sections. If a fabric appears in or near the center of a quilt and is never used again, or if a fabric not used before is introduced in the final border, it would suggest that one ran out of fabric and *had* to use something else. That may, in fact, be the case, but there are ways to integrate the fabrics so the shortage will not look obvious.

If there is a particular piece of fabric that you feel *must* be used in the center, but you have only a very small piece, and no more is available, then save just enough to use a few small bits in the outer edges of the quilt. Or, if near the completion of the top, you find a new fabric that is perfect for the final border (nothing else will do), choose some area near the center where as little as one piece could be replaced with the new fabric. Even such a small touch may be all that is needed to tie everything together.

As I said earlier, a general rule is to try to introduce all of the fabrics within the first major section of the quilt. Then when they appear again, it will be by design and not as an afterthought.

The question of how many fabrics to use in a medallion quilt is frequently raised. To answer this is difficult because there are no hard and fast rules, and tastes differ widely. Once when a student insisted, "Well, *about* how many?", I answered, "It all depends on the design of your quilt and the feeling you are trying to convey." She persisted by saying, "Yes, but surely you can give *some* idea." So I finally said, "Between five and 20 different fabrics." If less than five are used, there may be too little opportunity for flexibility in the transition from one section of the quilt to another. If there are more than 20 different fabrics, it might be difficult to incorporate them all into the central motif and also to integrate them successfully in the outer sections.

Background Fabrics

Varying the background fabric in a medallion quilt is an effective way to make it more interesting or to create the illusion of depth. If the same background is used throughout, the impression given is that of one large piece of fabric with smaller pieces laid on top. By alternating background fabrics in the different sections of a quilt, a more appealing effect is created, as can be seen in the two diagrams in fig. 49. Notice also how the different backgrounds add another dimension of interest to Lena Behme's *Shenandoah*, page 126, Ellen Swanson's *Star Variable* and Colleen Gosling's *New York Beauty*, page 86 and Ellie Bennett's *Star Surrounded*, page 98.

Fig. 49.

Poinsettia Medallion, pieced medallion quilt made by Fay Goldey, June, 1978-July, 1979. The central motif is an original design. The white area has poinsettia flowers quilted with stippling as a background. 85″ square.

Rosewood, pieced medallion quilt top made by Connie Gunn in 1981. The central medallion is a five-patch pattern based on the *Tree of Paradise* design. The batik fabric is reminiscent of the coloring and grain of rosewood. 80″ square.

Feathered Star Medallion, pieced medallion quilt made by Fay Goldey, March, 1980-April, 1982. 85″ square.

Barbara's Rose Fandangle, pieced medallion quilt top made by Barbara M. Kirkconnell, March, 1981-April, 1982. 88″ square.

Robin's Star, pieced medallion quilt made by Kathryn Kuhn, December, 1980-April, 1982. The quilt was made as a wedding present for Kathryn's daughter, Robin. The *Rising Star* pattern inspired the design. 86½" x 102½".

104

The choice of background fabrics depends primarily on the main design elements in the quilt and, perhaps, the type of quilting to be used. For example, elaborate fine quilting, stippling, stuffed work or trapunto shows up best on all white, muslin or other light solid colors. Therefore, one of these would be an appropriate choice for areas to be filled with fancy quilting.

Careful thought must be given to prints when they are used as background fabrics. Any print that is behind an appliquéd or patchwork design must be unobtrusive and should not detract from the main design. However, if a background fabric is needed to fill large areas containing no design elements, then the overall appearance of a quilt may be enhanced by a large print composed of paisleys or florals. A fabric with a regular pattern or strict geometric placement used in large areas may be distracting. It is better to use ones with an overall pattern.

Dark Center

By analyzing countless medallion quilts and through my teaching, I have begun to recognize certain factors common to nearly all appealing designs. One of these is the use of a *dark* fabric at the very center of the medallion. As with anything there are exceptions, and these will be discussed later. In most instances, however, if the center is light, it gives the illusion of a hole in the middle of the quilt. In fig. 50 the one on the left shows the light center and the hole it creates. However, the one on the right shows that with the simple addition of a small, diagonally set, dark square at the very center, a foundation is provided on which the whole design can grow. Another example of this is shown in two photographs of Pat McLaughlin's quilt on the next page. In

Fig. 50.

105

A Thousand and One Nights, pieced medallion quilt top made by Pat McLaughlin, May, 1979-April, 1982. This version shows how a "hole" is created when there is a light square in the center. Virginia, 84″ x 100″.

By putting a dark square in the center of the quilt and the center of the border motifs, Pat has achieved a stronger design.

the first photograph a light patch has been placed over the very center of the design and over some of the centers of the motifs in the borders. This creates the illusion of a hole in the middle of the design. The second photograph shows the quilt as it has been constructed with dark fabric forming a strong base at the center of the quilt.

What then is the explanation for quilts such as Judy Spahn's *Eclipse* (page 85), Fay Goldey's *Poinsettia* (page 103) or my own *Suzi's Box* (page 120)? All of these have light centers yet do not give the impression of a hole in the middle of the quilt. In both *Eclipse* and *Suzi's Box*, muslin is the accent or spark and does not serve as the base or background. Thus, one might conclude that when the background is dark and the center light, as is the case with these two quilts, the light center seems to project forward rather than to recede. However, when there is a light background fabric and the center, too, is light, it looks as though a hole has been cut through the center to the background with a resulting lack of substance.

And so to the remaining question of Fay Goldey's *Poinsettia*, which has both a light background and a light center. I think the key here is the design element. The central motif has an almost snowflake appearance, and one expects a snowflake to be lacy and to have open spaces in it. Despite the occasional exceptions, it seems safe to say that a dark beginning in the center of a quilt creates a base upon which the quilt can expand and, in general, lends substance to the overall appearance.

Dark Edge

Just as most medallion quilts seem more effective with a dark beginning they also seem to benefit from a dark ending. If the final border is composed of the darker fabrics used in the quilt, it acts like a stopping place—like the frame around a picture. Light borders often appear to leave the quilt open-ended, in need of another fabric to complete the quilt. Once again there are exceptions. As I was designing and constructing my *Blue Star Sapphire* quilt, I was trying to adhere to all the so-called rules I felt I had arrived at concerning a successful medallion design. However, many did not work. For instance, I kept thinking I would need a dark outer edge, yet as I finished the quilt I realized the only ending that worked was the same light border that had been used throughout the quilt. With most quilts a dark border or fabric used throughout serves as the emphasis for the quilt. However, my quilt almost seemed to be a negative of most quilts, and the light border was the strongest factor. Anything else used around the final edge was insignificant. This is yet another example illustrating that there are no hard and fast rules in medallion quiltmaking—only possible guidelines.

Amount of Fabric to Purchase

One of the questions I am asked repeatedly is: How much fabric should be bought for a medallion quilt? That is very difficult to answer because it is almost impossible to know in advance exactly which fabrics are going to work best in different parts of a quilt. Furthermore, all too often (and I know this from experience!) the colors of an entire quilt may be coordinated around a special piece of fabric; then when the time comes to introduce that fabric, it just is not right and has to be set aside.

Because most of us share a lack of unlimited funds and storage space, I can offer a few general comments to serve as guidelines when decision time comes at the fabric counter. For me the best way to work with colors and fabrics in a medallion quilt is to have a large variety of fabrics at my disposal. If I see a fabric I like but do not have use for immediately, I buy some of it anyway. You never know just which piece will be the perfect choice in a particular situation until the time comes to try it.

If I know ahead of time that a specific design, flower or figure will be centered in a patchwork piece, it will probably be necessary to purchase an additional amount of yardage. In my *Blue Star Sapphire* quilt, the same flowers are centered throughout in the eggplant-colored triangles that form the small pieced border. Because those flowers were printed about six inches apart on the fabric, almost five yards were needed in order to cut enough identical triangles.

In general, three yards of any one fabric is a fairly safe amount to purchase, particularly if several different fabrics are being used in a quilt. If the fabric is to serve as an accent or spark, one yard should be plenty. An accent, if used more than sparingly, tends to be both overwhelming and distracting in a quilt. So much depends on the design. However, for background fabrics and large prints it is important to buy lengths of at least three yards.

Border stripes must be considered in a different way. As noted previously, a border stripe should be used at least twice in a quilt, and in all probability more often than that. Therefore, the amount to purchase depends upon how many times the stripe is repeated in the fabric and how often it might be used in the quilt. Some fabrics have the same stripe repeated consistently across the width; in others, three or four different stripes may alternate so that each one is repeated only three or four times. To give you an idea of the amount you may need, the light-colored border stripe in my *Blue Star Sapphire* quilt came from a French fabric that my friend Soizik Labbens sent me. The stripe was repeated only three times and I ended up using 33 running yards, which meant I needed 11 yards of fabric. In general, plan to have at least 30 running yards of a border stripe if it is to be used as a printed border in a medallion quilt. If the fabric is printed with only one stripe repeated throughout, three yards should be ample. However, if the stripe you wish to use appears only three times, then a length of ten yards would be necessary. An ideal situation would be to find a friend who wants to use one of the other stripes and is willing to divide the fabric.

The most important thing to keep in mind is to remain flexible and to be prepared to make changes. Accept the fact that even though certain fabrics were purchased specifically for your quilt, you may not use all of them. Try not to worry ("My husband is going to kill me if I don't use this fabric in my quilt.") or get hung up ("By golly, I bought it and I'm going to use it!").

Also, bear in mind that the amounts I have recommended may be more than you will actually need, but they should spare you the disaster of running short before your quilt is completed. Remember, too, that if you are hooked on quilting the way many of us are, a temporarily discarded fabric enlarges your stash available for future projects.

Running short of a certain fabric isn't the worst that can happen either. Such a situation can force your mind to work overtime on a solution that may prove far more interesting than the original plan. In my *Ray of Light* medallion quilt (page 157), the large print used throughout came from a 2½-yard piece of Indonesian batik, and there was no way of getting any more of that. I had planned to use it in the large triangle in the outer edge of the quilt, just as it had been used in the large triangles around the center. I tried every other fabric I had used in the quilt and not one looked right; that fabric *had* to be used in the outer border. Finally the realization came to me that the whole triangle did not have to be made of the batik print—as long as a piece of it was used. I decided upon a small triangle of batik bordered by two other fabrics and found to my delight that it looked even better than triangles made up entirely of batik.

Eight-Pointed Star Medallion made by Diane Haley-Smith, September, 1978-March, 1979. Maryland, 91" square.

Constructing A Medallion Quilt

Once the outline has been prepared and decisions have been made about the center motif, general colors and fabrics, you are ready to begin. The mechanics of constructing a medallion quilt are not complicated; in fact, there is probably less sewing involved than on a block-style quilt. However, it seems to be more difficult and to take longer because of the mental process that one must go through—the thinking time between the sections. With most traditional block-style quilts, once decisions are made about colors, fabrics, size of block and placement of fabrics, the pieces can be cut out and no further planning is required until one comes to the border. With a medallion quilt new decisions are required at each step of the way.

When I work on a medallion quilt, after one part is decided upon and the pieces are cut out, I am usually so anxious to see what it will look like that I rush to get it finished; then there comes another long period of agonizing over what the next step will be. For someone like myself who likes to have some relaxing hand sewing to do in the evening, a medallion quilt hardly serves the need. I end up doing more thinking than sewing.

There also seems to be a lot more taking out with a medallion quilt or, as my friend Ellen Swanson puts it "piecing and pitching." Often I find myself taking apart something that just isn't right even though it seemed like it would work before it was sewn. I try ahead of time to cut fabrics and lay them out to get a general idea, but they never look the same as when they are actually pieced together.

If you are not satisfied, *don't* continue. Why spend another year on a project that you are unhappy with when an extra few hours of work might make it just right? I became so discouraged when piecing my *Blue Star Sapphire* quilt that I almost discarded it completely. I kept replacing pieces that did not look right until finally only five fabrics remained of the 14 that were in the original center. However, I am glad I persevered. I would not have been able to finish the project unless I was happy with it.

Drafting the Pattern

If you have the outline for your quilt sketched out, have the fabrics in hand and have determined the central motif, then you are ready to begin drafting.

It is almost impossible to use ready-made patterns to construct a medallion quilt. The chances are slim of finding the design in the exact size you need, and if you have altered a traditional pattern or designed your own, there would not be a pattern available anyway. Furthermore, to adhere rigidly to ready-made patterns would not allow the adaptability that is needed.

The whole quilt should not be drafted all at once. Work from the center outward, drafting each new section only as you come to it. You may find when one section is complete that it needs the addition of another border or strip of fabric that had not been planned initially. This would change the size of the parts that follow, and if everything had been drafted in advance you would lose the flexibility needed to make the changes.

If the center motif is very large and you cannot find paper big enough, try drafting only one quarter of the design. My first book, *Patchwork Patterns*, shows how to make patterns in any size and gives guidelines for creating original designs. Anyone unfamiliar with drafting may find it beneficial to read that book before beginning construction.

Making Templates

Templates are pattern pieces that are used to cut out the design. Unlike dress patterns, they should be cut from a sturdy material with firm edges. The template is held down with one hand while the other hand draws around it. Use a pencil or other washable marker that will show up yet not ruin the fabric. In a quilt, many pieces are usually cut from the same pattern piece, and if the material used for the templates is not sturdy, the edges soon fray.

My favorite template material is transparent plastic. There are several varieties available to purchase and some to recycle, such as old x-ray film, plastic bacon wrappers or plastic lids. I prefer using a slightly abrasive plastic because it doesn't slip easily on the fabric. Seam allowances, grain lines, names of pattern pieces, etc. can be marked on the plastic with a permanent ink pen.

I prefer transparent plastic to cardboard or sandpaper for several reasons. First, being able to see through the template makes it easier to center designs on the fabric; second, using plastic eliminates some of the possibilities of error. For instance, if an opaque material such as cardboard is used, each piece must first be cut from the paper pattern and then transferred to the cardboard for cutting again. Each of these cuttings may slightly alter the shape of the template and could change the overall size of the pieces, causing difficulty in accurately completing the design. One of the cuttings can be eliminated by using clear plastic. You simply lay it over the design and, using a ruler, draw the lines directly onto the plastic, then cut. But no matter what material is used, extreme care must be taken to insure that the template is *accurate*.

One-fourth inch is commonly added to each piece for the seam allowance. There are basically two methods to use. One is to add the quarter inch directly to the template so that the pencil line is the cutting line. If this method is used you must "eyeball" the sewing line or mark another line for use for stitching.

The second method is to cut the template the size of the finished piece. The pencil line is used for sewing, and each piece is cut one-quarter inch from the line. I prefer to use the first method, but it is strictly a matter of personal preference.

When making templates for pieces with very sharp points like the *Mariner's Compass*, the quarter-inch allowance extends outwards way beyond the actual seam. I prefer to cut the point off one-fourth inch from the tip of the seam line to eliminate the bulk of extra long points. (See fig. 51.)

To eliminate confusion it helps to number each template to correspond to numbers of each piece on the design. If the grain of the fabric needs to go a certain way, you may also want to mark that on the template with an arrow.

Cutting out the Quilt

Once the center design of the medallion quilt is drafted and the templates are made, you are ready to cut out the pieces. First, the fabric should be prewashed in lukewarm water with a mild soap to allow excess dye to wash out and to eliminate the possibility of shrinkage at a later time. It can then be placed in a dryer or on a line to dry. If wrinkled, it should be pressed.

Sometimes when using a solid-color fabric or one with no definite design, I will cut out two pieces at a time. However, trying to cut more than two could cause the fabric to slip and could distort the shape. To insure accuracy and also enable you to center fabric designs within the pattern pieces, it is better to cut each piece individually.

The direction in which the templates are placed upon the fabric is very important. This varies depending upon the design and the arrangement of the shapes within the design. The most crucial consideration is the grain lines and biases of the fabric and where they lie on the various pieces. Wherever possible, plan to have the straight edges of the fabric fall along the *outer* edges of each section in the unit, block or quilt. This eliminates any distortion in the block. Do not worry about putting the biases next to straight edges. It is much more important to have either the lengthwise or crosswise grain of the goods along the outside edges of the work. If the biases fall along the outer edges, they will stretch out of shape and cause the block to be wavy. The triangle shown in fig. 52 could either be cut with the

Fig. 51.

Fig. 52.

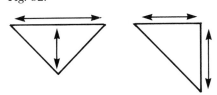

Fig. 53.

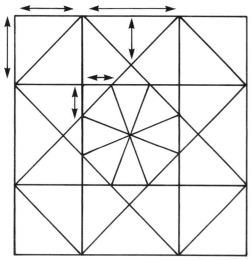

grain along the two short sides or with it along the long side, depending on the placement of the triangle within the pattern.

In the design in fig. 53 the triangles at the corners and those along the middle edges are exactly the same size and shape, but should be cut differently. The corner ones should be cut with the straight on the two short sides and the bias on the long side; the middle ones should be cut exactly opposite with the bias on the two short edges and the straight on the longer edge. The smaller triangles of that same shape in the corners of the center square should be cut with the bias on the long edge.

When piecing a square composed of four triangles, the triangles should be cut with all the inner edges along the bias and the outer ones along the straight of the fabric. (Fig. 54.)

In pieced borders it is extremely important to have the straight grain of the fabrics along the *edges* of the border strip; otherwise the biases would cause the border to stretch way beyond its true length. A lot of easing would have to be done in order to get it to fit properly along the side of the quilt. The border designs in fig. 55 have arrows indicating where the grain should be placed.

Cutting diamonds for an eight-pointed star or points for *Mariner's Compass* type designs is different. For the most part those shapes should be cut with the grain going up the middle of the piece. (See fig. 56.)

Fig. 54.

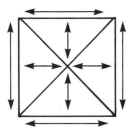

Fig. 55.

114

Fig. 56.

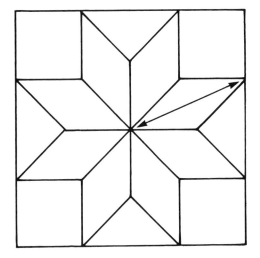

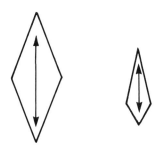

Fig. 57.

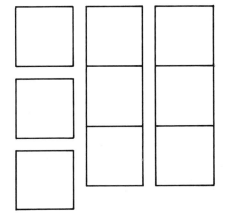

Piecing the Quilt

When the center design is cut out you will be ready to begin piecing. Whether the sewing is done by hand or by machine is up to you. I enjoy the relaxation that comes from sitting quietly and doing handwork, and I make my quilts entirely by hand. Trying to do intricate piecing on the sewing machine makes me frustrated and nervous. About the only time I have to sew on my quilts is in the evening when I would rather have the company of my family than be stuck in my sewing room. I also sew when I am traveling, sitting in doctor's offices or attending children's sports activities. Though I feel I can get better accuracy with hand sewing many quilters do an excellent job of piecing intricate work by machine and feel frustrated doing handwork. The important thing, whether it is done by hand or machine, is to make the work as precise and as neat as possible.

Just as I like to use 100% cotton fabric, I prefer 100% cotton thread. For appliqué, a size 50 mercerized cotton seems to work best. For hand piecing my favorite is a heavy-duty thread (usually available in drapery departments), which does not break as easily as a standard cotton. It also seems to be as sturdy as quilting thread without being quite so thick and bulky. Use a thread the color of one of the two fabrics that are being sewn together. If there is a sharp contrast between the thread and the fabric, the stitches will show along the seams on the front of the quilt. Seeing dark colored fabrics sewn together with light thread or vice versa can be very distracting. Sometimes a neutral shade can be found that will blend in with most of the fabrics, but it is usually best to change the color of thread to match the colors of the fabrics.

The piecing is done with a single thread cut to about 18 inches. A longer thread will have a tendency to knot and break more quickly. I prefer using a small, sturdy needle—usually a "between", size nine or ten. Thinner needles glide through the fabric more readily. However, you should choose a size that is the most comfortable for you.

It is sometimes difficult to thread such a small needle because the eye is proportionally small. The thread will go through the eye easier if it is cut at an angle, rather than blunt across.

The manner in which you go about piecing is entirely dependent upon the design and how it is laid out. It is best to piece *in units*, trying to have straight seams wherever possible. A simple nine-patch design is pieced in rows and then the rows are sewn together. (See fig. 57.)

One important thing to keep in mind when doing any hand piecing is to keep the seams free, and not to sew across them. In other words, as you approach a seam, lift it up and put the needle through its base. Continue sewing, leaving the seam free so that later it can lie in one direction or the other. One reason for doing this is that it makes it easier to get tight stitches where seams join, thereby keeping them together and preventing any holes. Keeping the seams free also aids in making sharp points and in getting corners to match.

In order to get the points to meet neatly in a design where several come together, follow fig. 58.

Fig. 58a. Sew together half of the pieces and set them aside; then sew the other half, making sure that you have joined the pieces together tightly where the points come together. Each section should look like this from the front.

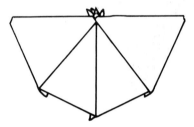

Fig. 58b. Next, with right sides together, match up the center points perfectly and use a pin to hold them in place.

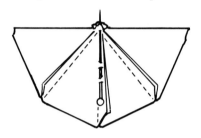

Fig. 58d. Sew up to the seam line, making sure not to catch any of the seams in the stitches. Do several backstitches right at the center and then pass the needle through the *base* of the seam line: now pull all the seams to the right, do a couple more backstitches, and continue sewing across.

Fig. 58c. Begin sewing and, as you approach the center, take out the pin and pull the seams towards the left.

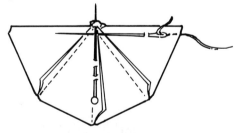

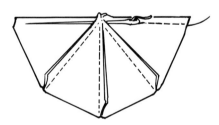

As long as you take care to match the points, sew in units, and are sure to take only the amount of seam allowance that was planned, you should have no trouble piecing your design. Sometimes with a more complex pattern, however, it is difficult to figure out the simplest way to break it down into units.

Fig. 59. **Castle Keep** (eight-point star category). Designed by Jinny Beyer, 1979.

A more complicated pattern like *Castle Keep* would be constructed by following figs. 59a through 59e. Piecing the design in this manner eliminates having to pivot because all of the sewing is done with straight seams.

Fig. 59a. Begin with the very center by sewing the first four triangles together and then the second four. Next with right sides together take one long seam across the middle. Be sure to match the corners and not to sew across the seams as explained opposite.

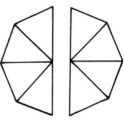

Fig. 59b. A square is formed next by sewing four small triangles to the center octagon.

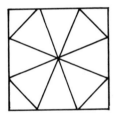

Fig. 59c. Third, piece four identical sections as shown below.

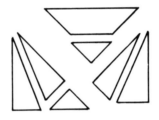

Fig. 59d. The corner units are made next.

Fig. 59e. And finally they are put together in rows.

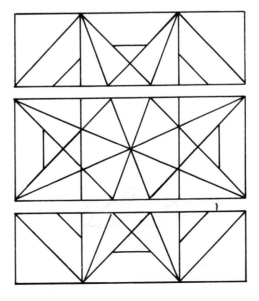

Fig. 60. **Mariner's Compass** (curved designs category). *Ladies' Art Company*, 1898.

I am often asked how to get sharp points when constructing such designs as the center of my *Ray of Light* quilt or other sunburst patterns. There is no big secret. It is all in the order in which the pieces are put together. Following the sequence described below for *Mariner's Compass*, fig. 60, should eliminate any problems with piecing it or similar patterns.

Fig. 60a. First sew the smallest points (2) around the center circle (1). By folding the circle and marking off eighths it is easy to gauge the distance between each point and get them on evenly.

Fig. 60b. Second, sew four of the largest points (3) into the center section as shown. Start at the edge of the point and sew right to the circle and, without cutting the thread, pivot the point and sew up the other side.

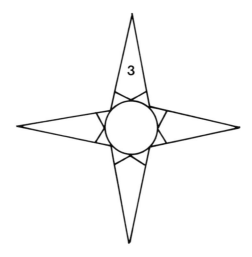

Fig. 60c. Now set the center aside and start working from the outside in. Piecing in units, start with the smallest point (4) and make a wedge by adding a background piece (5) to either side. Do this on all sixteen of the smaller points.

When working with a design with so many points radiating from the center, there is a possibility that the finished block will not lie flat—it might either ruffle or cup inward. There is a way to overcome that problem, but it takes a little extra work. Go to the original drawing of the design and make a new template that

is the size of the wedge-shaped pieces just sewn (one of the smaller points with the two background pieces on either side). Add the seam allowance around the whole shape and check to be sure that the wedges are the same size as the template. If not, either let some seams out or take some in until they are the correct size. If all the pieces correspond to the template now, they should lie flat when the block is complete. It is a lot easier to make adjustments to the seams before the block is sewn together.

Fig. 60d. Next go to the medium-size points (6) and sew one of the smaller wedges to either side. You will now have eight new larger wedges. Once again go to the original drawing and make a still larger template, this time incorporating the medium-size points and the wedges on either side. Check the eight new wedge-shaped pieces to be sure that they are the correct size.

118

Fig. 60e. Now go to the four large points that were not set into the center section and sew one of the eight wedges to either side of them. Make another template to check as before.

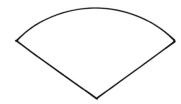

Fig. 60f. Finally, go back to the center section and sew the four large wedges between the points.

Fig. 60g. The last step is to sew the corner pieces (7) onto the circle.

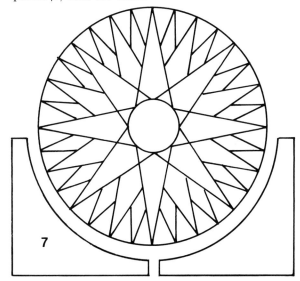

These are just two examples of the order in which to sew more complicated patterns. I hope they will help you to analyze your own design and see how best to break it up for piecing.

After the central motif is complete, you are ready to start the next part of the quilt. Working from the outline, you can plan borders or other plain, pieced or appliqué areas as necessary. It helps to be able to pin the center to a wall so that you can stand way back and take a good look. Try different designs and fabrics around the center until you find the ones that work best. If there is time, it also helps to take photographs and study the pictures. You may notice something in a photograph that you might otherwise miss.

Support groups also help. If you have a friend or group of friends who are making medallion quilts, it is beneficial to get together and talk about them. The positive feedback that comes from sharing is amazing and adds new ideas to the concepts of quilt design. Someone says something that sparks an interesting thought and that in turn leads to something else and before long the right solution is reached.

Suzi's Box, pieced medallion quilt made by Jinny Beyer in 1975. The piece added along one side shows the original border that was planned, and was too overpowering.

Planning and Executing Borders

Medallion quilt borders have one of these purposes: to complement, strengthen, or complete the design. The idea of incorporating many different borders into the quilt is tempting; however, giving continuity is more important than variety. Each part of the quilt design should be a link to another, and the frequent introduction of a completely new border would confuse rather than integrate. Therefore, every addition must be carefully and thoughtfully planned.

Just as one normally wouldn't choose a frame before having the picture for it, one does not plan a border before finishing the central design of the quilt. Though the approximate width for each border may be sketched in the outline, it is best to wait, as I have said repeatedly, until each section of the quilt is finished before going on to the next. Taking time and planning in stages can save you much anguish and repeated work.

When I made *Suzi's Box*, opposite, I had planned the entire quilt before I ever began piecing it. Most of the center section was complete, so I took along an outer border to work on while I was on vacation. Upon my return, I laid it all out on the floor—only to find that the border I had pieced was overwhelming. It spoiled the overall look of the quilt. My mistake was in following to the letter my preplanned diagram. On an 8 x 10 piece of paper the border looked perfect; but when transferred into fabric the proportions were altered entirely. In the second photograph of *Suzi's Box*, a portion of that first border has been placed over the quilt. It is obvious that it would not have been effective. I set the border aside and later used it to make several wall hangings and other small projects.

Now when I plan a border it usually takes many days and endless polling of family and friends as to the best combinations. I waste fabric at this stage because the only way I can be sure something will be right is actually to see it. I cut various shapes and lay them next to the adjoining areas. Sometimes I may even have to piece part of the design before I am certain of how it will look.

Border Design

Types of borders to consider are pieced, appliquéd, plain fabric or a printed border stripe. You may also want to plan a decorative border to be added later with quilting. It is best to use more than one type; using the same one throughout makes the quilt monotonous. A pieced border might be used interchangeably with a fabric or appliqué border. There are many possibilities. The main consideration is that no border should stand alone. Each should be used at least twice, and if used only once, then it should be a strong reflection of some other part of the quilt. For instance, Ann McClintic has used the small black and white triangle border in four different places in her quilt on page 66 to provide unity. The outer border, which is between two rows of those triangles, has not been used before. However, it comprises elements that strongly echo the center part of the quilt, providing a perfect balance.

Whatever the type of border used, it should reflect something already contained in the quilt. A printed fabric border may pick up the colors used previously; a pieced border may adapt a shape or design segment from another portion of the quilt; an appliquéd or quilted border could also repeat part of the design of the central medallion, or perhaps a motif in one of the fabrics used.

Proportion of the borders as they relate to the center and to each other is very important to good designing. If they are too wide, the center will be overwhelmed; too narrow and they are lost and insignificant. It is important also to vary the *width* of the different border areas. If each new section is the same width or close to it, the overall impact can be monotonous. It is much better to balance smaller areas with larger areas. The diagrams in figs. 61, 62, 63 and 64 show two versions of two different outlines, but in those on the left the designs are static because the borders are approximately the same size. The variation in the width of the borders in the diagrams on the right make them much more interesting.

Deciding which type of design to use in a border is difficult. Perhaps the most important thing to keep in mind is to try to repeat a shape or motif from the central part of the quilt. For example, if squares and triangles are used in the center, then repeat them in the border. Do not introduce circles unless you plan to integrate the angles and curves effectively throughout. Do not plan an appliquéd border if all the rest of the quilt is pieced. If, for instance, the central motif is based on an eight-pointed star, the borders could reflect diamonds from the star, as Diane Smith has done in her quilt shown on page 110. She echoed her central motif by using smaller versions of the *Eight-Pointed Star* in the border. She has also made a border of diamonds which are the same shape as the diamonds in the star.

Fig. 61.

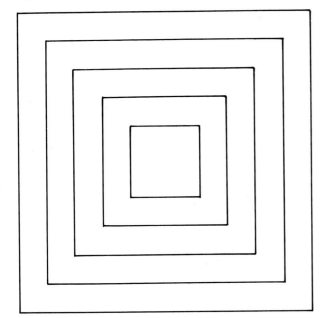

Fig. 62.

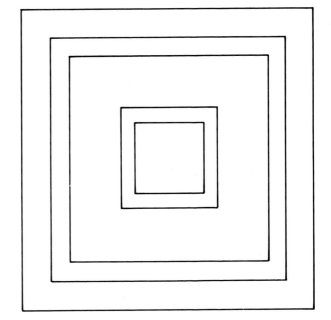

Fig. 63.

Fig. 64.

123

Fig. 65. **Mariner's Rose** (eight-pointed star category). Designed by Jinny Beyer for the 1982 Sea Pines Seminar.

Two more designs that could be used as central motifs appear here (figs. 65 and 66) along with borders that have been made by taking actual shapes or sections from the main design.

If a shape from the central motif is being used to create a border, the size of that shape is critical. It should be equal to or smaller than the piece it is echoing. Shapes that are too large in proportion to the center are overpowering. That was one of the problems with the disaster border I had originally planned for *Suzi's Box*.

Fig. 66. **Star Sapphire** (eight-pointed star category). Designed by Jinny Beyer for the 1981 Sea Pines Seminar.

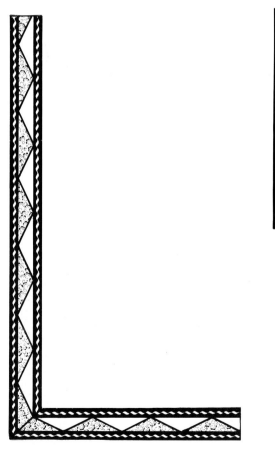

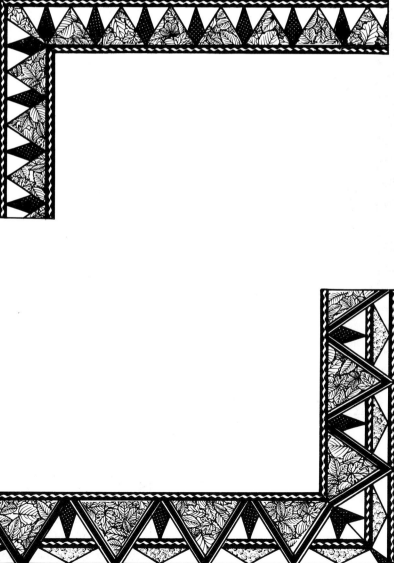

125

Shenandoah, pieced medallion quilt made by Lena Behme, Spring, 1978- Summer, 1979. The traditional blocks, *Delectable Mountains* and *Autumn Leaves,* reminded Lena of country property she and her husband own; and she presented the quilt to him as a 30th wedding anniversary gift. Virginia, 92″ square.

With many medallion quilts, I think it is important for the final section of the quilt to exhibit a strong reflection of the central motif. Try this experiment. Take strips of paper and cover the outer border on Lena Behme's quilt above. The whole balance of the design is lost. By repeating the *Sawtooth* from the center in the outer section, Lena has united all the segments of the quilt. Without the final border, the center *Sawtooth* design has no reason for existing because it forms no link with any other design element in the quilt. Try the same experiment on other quilts pictured in the book.

Some of the photographs will show another border treatment frequently seen and effectively used—that of incorporating miniature versions of the central design into blocks framing the quilt. Another possibility is the use of only a portion of the design, perhaps a quarter or half section, as seen in the *Mariner's Compass* border below (fig. 67) or as Barbara Kirkconnel and Marilyn Titman have done in their respective quilts on pages 103 and 83.

Earlier I noted the importance of usually using a dark fabric to surround the outer edges of a quilt. Likewise, it seems advisable to have the heaviness of a design toward the outside. For example, some borders, such as *Dog Tooth* (fig. 68), have triangles that can be pointing either inward or outward depending upon the border placement. Generally, if points near the inner part of a medallion quilt are directed outward, they help the eye travel beyond the center. However, those same points used around the outer edge and directed inward help contain the design and dictate an end to the quilt.

Look at the *Dog Tooth* border in Betty Larson's quilt on page 84. All the triangles point outward except in the last border where they are reversed, stopping the outward flow and ending the quilt. There are exceptions, of course, which only serve as another reminder that even though there are some basic guidelines, there are no hard and fast rules.

Sometimes a quilt needs breathing space or some calm areas between the designs. An elaborate border might be distracting. Experiment with plain or printed fabric borders as well as more complex ones. A very simple border used more than once may be the unifying factor in the entire quilt.

Fig. 67. *Mariner's Compass* border.

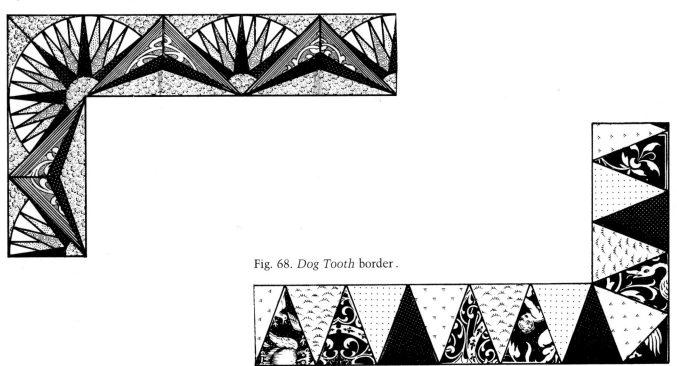

Fig. 68. *Dog Tooth* border.

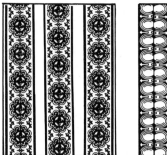

Fig. 69.

Fabric Borders

Fabric borders can be made by cutting pieces of cloth into strips. Some of the most attractive are those cut from decorative stripes. Once in a while a beautiful fabric will have the design printed diagonally. As tempting as it might be to cut such a print apart, I strongly urge against it. The bias edges would be impossible to work with. The only time this type of bias should be used would be for binding or for some types of appliqué work. In general, look for fabrics with one or more different stripes repeated across the width, and with the stripe running along the lengthwise grain of the fabric, as in the examples in fig. 69. It is also possible to make your own striped borders by sewing different pieces of fabric together. Look for fabrics that have the designs printed in straight rows. These rows can be cut apart and added to other strips of fabric to manufacture a border, as shown in fig. 70.

Fig. 70.

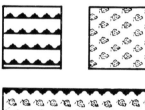

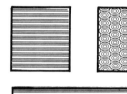

The use of printed fabric borders can add a unique dimension to medallion quiltmaking. I use two types, each in different ways. One is a border that is usually from three-fourths to three inches wide. When I began quiltmaking I used this type of border strictly to edge quilts or individual blocks. In recent years, however, I have discovered what a distinctive touch they can add when used within various parts of a design. Now I always try incorporating them into some part of each pattern I make as well as incorporating them around the outer edges of the block or sections of the quilt. Here are two examples (figs. 71 and 72) showing the difference with and without the use of printed borders inside the design.

Fig. 71. **Courtyard Square** (eight-pointed star category). Designed by Jinny Beyer, 1980).

Fig. 72. **Cross and Crown** (five-patch category). *Ladies' Art Company,* 1898.

The second type of border is a thin narrow strip (usually about a half-inch wide), which really serves as an outline more than an actual border. It can be used on either side of a printed, pieced or appliquéd border to add emphasis or definition. It can be used as a stop-gap between one piece of fabric and another border or fabric, or it can be used around a block or parts of a design as an outline. Used alone the outline strip would appear insignificant, too narrow, and would spoil the proportion and balance of the quilt. See the examples in fig. 73 with and without the use of an outline border.

Fig. 73. **Whirling Star,** (eight-pointed star category).*Virginia Snow Patchwork Designs,* ca. 1930.

My quilt *Blue Star Sapphire* uses the two types of fabric borders described earlier, both within the designs and around the edges of the various sections of the quilt. Study of the photograph of this quilt on page 65 may give you more ideas for the use of printed fabric borders.

As with other borders, it is best to repeat the use of fabric borders and not to introduce a new one each step of the way. Because using only one can be too constraining, I usually work with three or four and alternate them throughout the quilt. Remember that if several border prints are used, they must be compatible.

Measuring for Borders

People are not computers, and it would be virtually impossible to produce a quilt in which every single finished measurement was exactly the size as graphed or drafted. Fabrics tend to stretch and give, and seam allowances may be slightly off. If a block-style quilt was made from 10″ patterns and there were five blocks across the width and seven along the length, one would assume that the finished size would be 50″ x 70″, and it would seem logical to cut 50″ and 70″ border strips plus allowances for seams and mitering. However, it is entirely possible that each block might end up 9⅞″, making the finished size 49⅜″ x 69⅛″ and causing the borders, cut to fit 50″ x 70″, to ripple after being sewn.

Even though you may have drafted the pattern with extreme accuracy, you must *remeasure the quilt every step of the way* and recalculate the measurements of each new area as the quilt grows. *Never* piece the outer borders of the medallion quilt before the center is done. If you do, you may be in for a rude surprise.

While I was piecing my *Ray of Light* quilt (page 157), I wanted to have something easy to work on during vacation. So I set the unfinished center aside and started on the outer triangles with the *Sawtooth* piecing. According to my outline, the center would be 40″ and that would make the base of the triangles 10″. While away I finished all the triangles, and once home, I completed the center. Imagine my dismay when it ended up 39″ instead of 40″! Had all the outer triangles not already been pieced I could have recalculated the measurements and adjusted the size to fit. I ended up adding an extra half-inch border around the center section to compensate, but from that point on I have never worked ahead of myself and always wait to piece the borders until the preceding part is completed.

Just as important as step-by-step remeasurement of the quilt is *how* the measurement is taken. Most beginners lay the piece down and measure the edges, usually giving themselves a measurement longer than it should be because of the distortion caused by fabric biases and seams. As I have noted, using that larger measurement will cause the quilt to ruffle or wave.

The best place to measure for the correct size of the borders is across the *center* of the quilt. The same holds true whether you are measuring for a full-size quilt or something as small as a pillow top; or whether you are measuring for a fabric border or a pieced border. (See fig. 74.)

Try laying a pieced quilt top without any borders added to it on the floor; lift up the bottom two corners and bring them to the center. More often than not the measurement across the bottom edge will be wider than the one across the center, but the dimension across the center is the *true* measurement and the one to be used for determining the lengths of the border strips (fig. 75.).

Fig. 74.

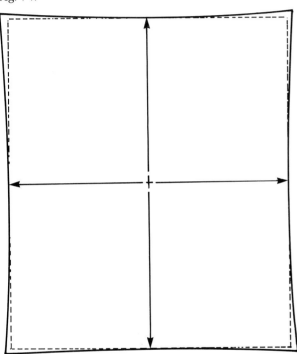

Fig. 75.

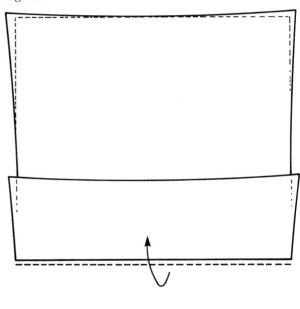

I have seen a difference of as much as 6″ between the two measurements, and that has been due strictly to stretching of bias edges or seams. As mentioned in chapter 4 on constructing the medallion quilt, this problem can be controlled by accurate cutting of the pieces and by keeping the straight of the fabric along the outer edges of the work. Be sure that fabric biases *never* fall on the outer edges of borders.

If there is a big difference between the measurement across the bottom of the quilt and the true measurement across the center, then the edges will have to be eased in to fit the border. Find the halfway point on both the border and the edge of the quilt; then pin them together. Pin their corners together; then find the midpoint of each half and pin those together. Continue until all the ease has been taken up. As the two pieces are sewn together be sure not to take any tucks; just ease the fullness in.

Fig. 76.

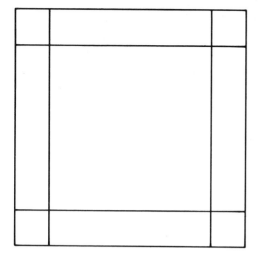

Fig. 77.

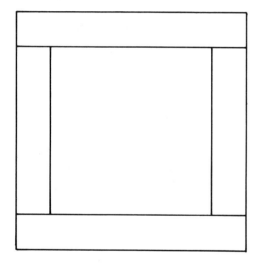

Fig. 78.

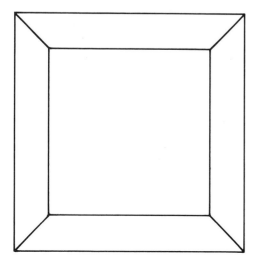

Mitering

When adding strips of fabric for borders, there are three ways to treat the corners: Add squares to them (fig. 76), overlap two of the corners (fig. 77), or miter them (fig 78). I usually prefer mitering, and although there are several methods, I use the following: Lay the strip of fabric to be used for the border across the *center* of the quilt (see fig. 79); smooth it into place so it is the same width as the quilt. By measuring right to the edge, the seam allowances will automatically be added because the allowance is already on the quilt top. Either fold the border down at right angles or use a 45° triangle to mark the angle; then cut the miter. Do the same on the opposite side, and if the quilt is square, use this strip as a pattern and cut three more exactly the same. If the quilt is rectangular cut only one more strip and repeat the process for the other two sides.

Fig. 79.

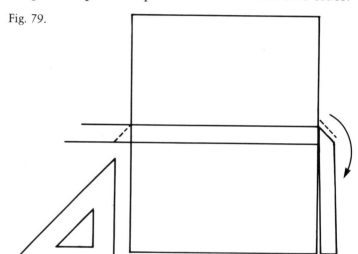

Next, sew all four strips onto the quilt, easing in any extra fullness, and finally sew the mitered edges. Sometimes the bias edges of the mitered strips will get pulled and distorted. Therefore, after sewing the miters go to the iron and press. The iron will smooth out any fullness that there might be. If the iron has pressed a tuck along the seam, go back and restitch along the crease line, and the border should be perfectly mitered. As long as you have taken the precaution of measuring across the *center* of the quilt it should lie flat, and the border should have no ruffled edges.

Corners

Most important to the success of any border are the corners and whether or not they turn the angle smoothly. If the four corners do not match or if the border is arbitrarily cut off when it gets to the edge, the entire quilt will be unbalanced. Although the central motif should be the focal point of the quilt, the eye will travel immediately to the corners if they are too bold or disjointed. An effective border must provide a symmetrical frame around the quilt. There are various ways to plan it so that its corners turn smoothly.

Fig. 80.

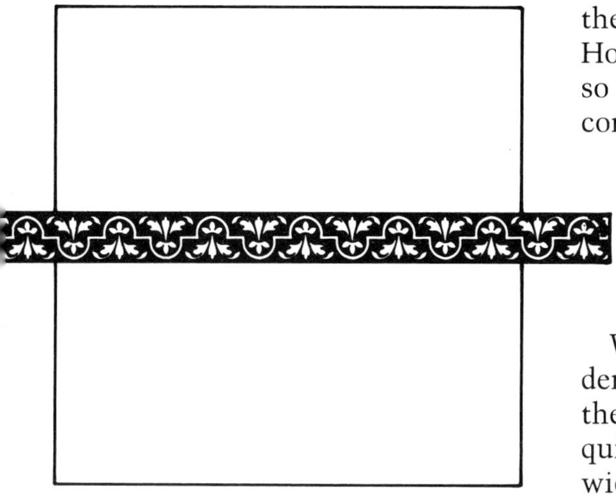

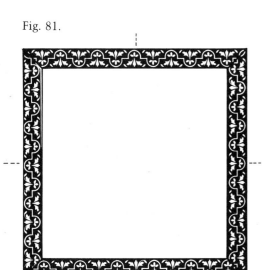

Border Prints   With pieced, appliqué or quilted borders there are mathematical ways to determine the proportions so that the corners turn smoothly. It is a matter of adjusting the size of the shapes to fit the length of the border. However, there is no way to change a design that is printed, so that getting those types of borders to match at the corners is more of a challenge.

Fig. 81.

When working with a square quilt, making the fabric borders turn is relatively easy. Find the center portion of one of the designs on the border and place that at the center of the quilt (fig. 80), making sure to have enough border for the width of the piece and the miter. (In order to get the correct measurement, remember to place the border across the *middle* of the quilt.) Next, miter the corners. If you have started in the middle of a design on the border, then the ends of each strip should also be identical. Make three more matching strips, using the one just cut as a guide. By making sure that the design on the border stripe is in exactly the same place on each side all of the corners will be uniform when the border is sewn on (fig. 81).

When a fabric with a definite shape or motif is used you may want to experiment to see which placement of the border looks best in terms of the design that will end up in the corner. For instance, with the border in fig. 81 an upward loop was placed at the center of the quilt, and in the one in fig. 82 a downward loop was used at the center. Each produces a different design at the corner.

Fig. 82.

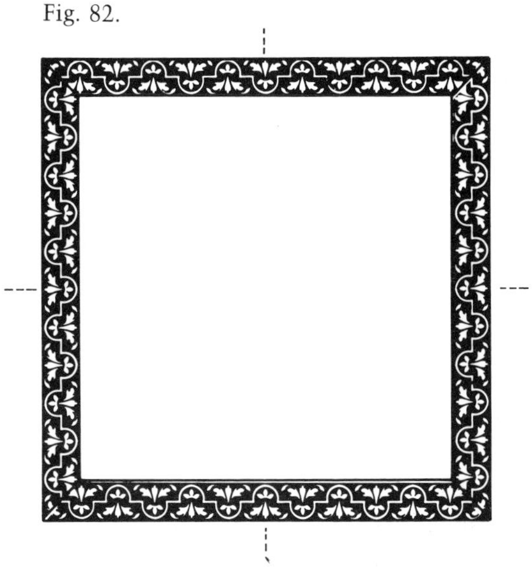

In rectangular quilts, with two of the edges a different length from the other two, the designs will not come out even at the corners unless you are very lucky. Experiment by trying different parts of the design at the center of the border until you find a corner match as close as possible. Remember always to place the *center* of the design at the *center* of the quilt so that the ends of the border will be matched. At this point, if the corners do not match it is necessary to do some fudging. As I have said, one of the first places the eye travels after leaving the center of the quilt is to the corners. Therefore it is far more important to have the corners look symmetrical than any other areas. Cut two of the border strips longer than necessary but no more than one inch longer if possible. Make sure they are cut at the corners exactly as the other two strips. Then take seams about ½-inch wide in unobtrusive parts of the design across the longer strips until they are the proper length. Unless you tell people the tucks are there they will never notice. It is probably very hard for you to find where I took the tucks along the printed borders in my *Blue Star Sapphire* quilt on page 65.

Fig. 83.

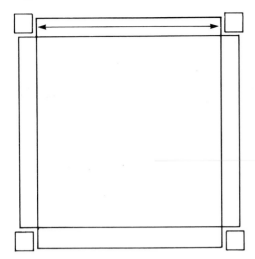

Pieced Borders Making a pieced border is easiest when the quilt is square because you need only to plan a border to fit one side and then copy it three times. When designing a border you can forget about the corner in the beginning. Measure and plan the border to go from edge to edge, and then plan a corner unit that will tie everything together (fig. 83). In order for the corner unit to work, the four border lengths must begin and end at the same place. That way a properly planned corner can just be inserted, and it will automatically connect the sides and form a smooth link around the corner.

With rectangular projects it is different. If you want the design of the borders to end in the same place on all sides (so the corner unit will fit), then you will have to figure mathematically how to do it. I tell how in detail later on in this chapter.

If the border is not planned to go continuously around the quilt, and you cannot get it to stop in the same place at all corners, there are other ways to deal with it. One possibility is to put squares in the corner of an entirely different design. Although this is not a very good solution, it is not so noticeable that the design of the border does not stop in the same place at all corners (fig. 84).

Fig. 84.

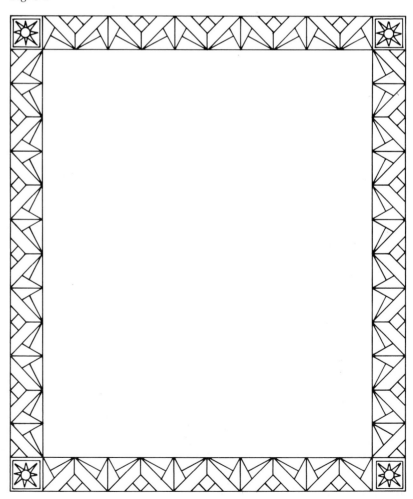

Fig. 85.

Fig. 86.

A better method, perhaps, is to work from the corners toward the center of the border and put a block or different design at the center (fig. 85). This method is preferable to the previous one because the corners are uniform, and it is not so noticeable that the designs do not meet at the same place in the center of the border as it is in the corners.

Another possibility is to have design areas interspersed with areas of plain or printed fabric. Boots Bartell has done this in her medallion quilt on page 86. In this way the length of the fabric can be adjusted along either side to allow the design areas to fit. See also the border design in fig. 86. The areas between the patched designs could be lengthened or shortened to allow the border to fit.

Drafting Pieced Borders to Fit

If the pieced border is to go unbroken continuously around the quilt, getting it to come out right at the corners can be a bit more difficult. Thank heavens for calculators! Before beginning the mathematics, design the unit for the corner and be sure it will connect properly with the sides of the quilt.

Often just another square unit of the border design will work for the corner piece, as in the small *Castle Wall* blocks that form the border in Nancy Johnson's quilt below. At other times you may have to plan something different for the corners as Barbara Kirkconnel has done in her quilt shown on page 103.

Navajo Sunset, pieced quilt top made by Nancy Johnson, 1979-1981. The turquoise, coral and brown colors reflect nature and earth and their importance to the Navajo way of life. Maryland, 93″ square.

Above:
Midnight Sun, pieced medallion quilt made by P. J. Wormington, January, 1981-April, 1982. 90″ square.

Above right:
Polaris, pieced medallion quilt made by Sandra C. Tucker, May, 1978-March, 1980. 108″ square.

Right:
Woodland Trails, pieced medallion quilt made by Eleanor Kastner, 1978-1979. 86″ square.

137

138

Opposite left:
California Beauty, pieced medallion wall quilt made by Darlene Shumway, completed in April, 1982. The central design is a variation of the *New York Beauty* design. 54″ square.

Opposite right:
Compromise, medallion wall quilt made by Susan McKelvey, 1978-1982. It is made of batik and cotton prints. Maryland, 69″ square.

Opposite below:
Blue Blazes, pieced medallion wall quilt made by Kathleen M. Lane, 1980-1982. All the diamonds and hexagons are cut from a striped border fabric and pieced together to form the shapes. Maryland, 48½″ square.

Most of the border diagrams drawn for this book show how to turn the corner. Study of the photographs will show you ways other quiltmakers have dealt with corners. You could also refer to my book, *The Quilter's Album of Blocks and Borders,* which has some 150 border designs, each showing a corner turn. Try experimenting with the shapes from your own design to develop a border with an interesting corner.

Borders based on geometric shapes are usually drafted in a grid of one or more squares. For instance, the *Sawtooth* border uses a grid of one square by one square, *Flying Geese* uses a grid of one square by two squares, and the *Nine Patch* border uses a grid of three squares (figs. 87, 88 and 89). The *size* of each square in the grid is determined by the length of the border and the number of individual squares that will be needed to fill the space. The *length* of each border strip is determined by the size of the quilt, thus that measurement is fixed. Therefore, you have to remain flexible about the *width* of the strip. In other words, if you decide that each square of the grid is going to be one inch, and the border design is *Sawtooth,* which requires only one square grid for the design, then the border would be one inch wide. If the design is *Flying Geese,* then the border would be two inches wide because that pattern requires a grid two squares deep.

Fig. 89.
Nine Patch
border.

Fig. 88. *Flying Geese* border.

Fig. 87. *Sawtooth* border.

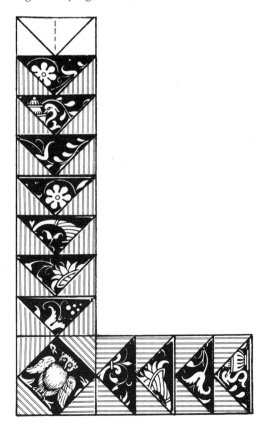

What if, according to your outline, the border needed to be four inches wide, yet the only way the pieced design could be worked out to fit was to make it two inches? A good solution would be to add a fabric border one inch wide on either side of the pieced design to make the border a total of four inches.

Some borders, such as *Flying Geese* and *Sawtooth*, have a specific direction. If they go in only one direction around the quilt, the corners will not be symmetrical (fig. 90).

Fig. 90.

When using this type of design, I find it more effective to change the direction of the border in the middle of the strips. That way the corners all look the same and the quilt looks balanced. The diagrams in fig. 91 show the same two borders used above, but with a reversal of direction in the middle of each border strip, so that the corners are uniform.

Fig. 91.

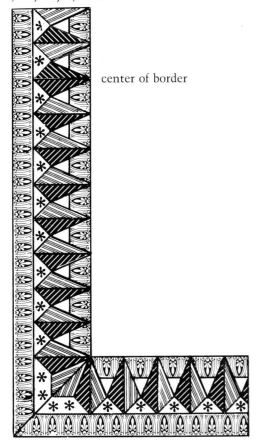

Fig. 92. *Castle Keep* border. Designed by Jinny Beyer, 1980.

center of border

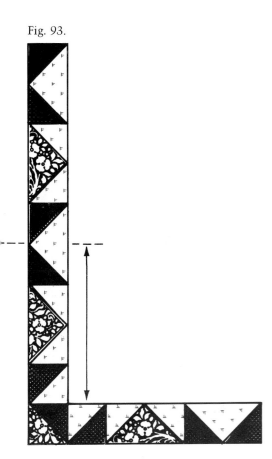

Fig. 93.

Many borders will require a reverse of direction, and it should be something to consider when planning your quilt designs. Mary Albright reversed the direction of the border that goes around the center of her medallion quilt shown on page 72 and Fay Goldey reversed the directions of both the *Sawtooth* and the arrow type border on her *Feathered Star Medallion* on page 103.

With a border such as *Castle Keep* in which the points are split and have a dark and a light fabric, the corners will not look balanced if the dark is always on the same side of the point. Although the pattern pieces themselves do not need to be reversed, designs such as these require a change of color in the middle of the border strips in order to have them look symmetrical at the corners (fig. 92). Study of Peggy Wormington's quilt on page 137 will show that she also had to reverse the color of the pieces on her outer border. Two dark pieces come together at the center of each side.

Getting a border to come out evenly at the corners requires careful planning. For example, when planning a border using the *Sawtooth* pattern, it will be necessary to have an even number of squares because that motif requires a change of direction in the middle of the border in order for it to turn the corners smoothly. If the area to be bordered is 42" square and you would like the width of the border to be approximately one inch, then a one-inch unit could be planned. Forty-two squares would fit on each side of the quilt. An extra one would then be added for each corner. If you want the border to be wider, then each square could be 1½", and 28 squares could fit along each side. A two-inch border would not work because there would be 21 squares along each side, and being an odd number it would not allow the design to reverse direction in the middle.

A rectangular design is a bit more difficult. If the quilt is 42" x 69", then a one-inch grid would not work because there would be 42 squares along one edge and 69 along the other, which would not allow the longer strip to reverse direction in the center of the border. However, if the grid were 1½", there could be 28 squares along one side and 46 along the other. It may take several minutes of trial-and-error figuring to come up with the number that will divide evenly into both sides of the quilt.

Some border patterns, however, use more than a one-square grid to make the design. In fig. 93, four squares are needed to allow the design to start and stop at the same place. In such a case, whatever the size of each square, the squares must be able to be grouped into multiples of four to fit along each side. If we now go back to the same 42" x 69" quilt, it is time to bring out the calculator again and find a size for the individual square that, when divided into either 42 or 69, will produce a number that is divisible by four. As it did in the previous example, 1½" won't work because, although 28 is divisible by four, 46 is not. Using 46 would leave two squares—or three inches—left over.

141

Often it is impossible to find a number that will come out perfectly along both sides of the quilt. That is when some adjustments will have to be made. The number that I found that worked the closest was 1.75″. Along the 42″ side it comes out perfectly at 24 squares or 6 four-inch units. Along the 69″ side it works out to 39.4 squares, which means you need another 0.6 of a unit, or approximately one inch. One way to get the extra length is to take slightly smaller seam allowances when piecing the border along that side and in this way "stretch" the border with the extra inch needed. If the border is too long, then slightly larger seam allowances can be taken to pull it in. When there is as little as one-inch difference, I find it easiest to adjust via the seam allowance. When working with a larger border unit, however, it is sometimes impossible to find a number to divide evenly or one with just a small difference. You could be confronted with as much as a two- to four-inch difference. If this happens, it is best to draft two completely different size border units, one to fit each side. Make sure not to vary the width of the borders, only the length, or else you would have two sides with a narrower border than the other two, and they would not meet at the corners. A 1/8-inch difference on a small shape spread over the length of the border could lengthen or shorten the border several inches. Yet, the fact that there is a difference in the size of the shapes on two sides of the quilt will most likely go unnoticed.

Border designs based on the eight-pointed star are not drafted in a grid of squares, and are therefore a bit more difficult. (For complete details on how to draft an eight-pointed star, see *Patchwork Patterns*, p. 89–99.) Let's say there is an eight-pointed star design in the center of the quilt and you want to use a border of diamonds taken from the star (fig. 94). The unit you would have to work with in order for the design to turn the corner smoothly is indicated by an arrow. It would also be necessary to reverse the color of the diamonds in the center of each side of the border in order for all of them to be symmetrical. Working with the same 42″ x 69″ measurements, after countless tries with the calculator, I finally decided that if the area for the border unit (shown between the arrows) was 4.245″, 9.88 units could be fit along the 42″ side and 16.23 units would fit along the 69″ side. Therefore, I would plan 10 units along one side and 16 along the other. That means that the border on the 42″ edge would be one-half inch too short and the one on the 69″ edge would be almost an inch too long. It would be necessary to make seam allowances a little larger along the longer sides of the quilt in order to pull them in one inch, and slightly smaller on the shorter sides to stretch them by one-half inch.

Now the big question: How does one draft a diamond the correct size to use in a 4.25-inch unit? The diamond from an eight-pointed star is not drafted using squares. To do

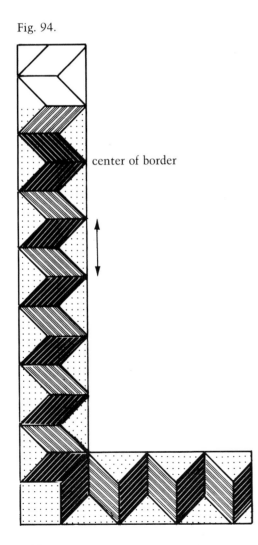

Fig. 94.

center of border

142

Fig. 95.

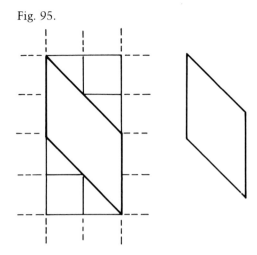

Fig. 96.

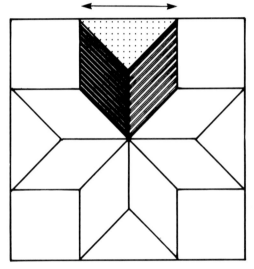

Fig. 97.

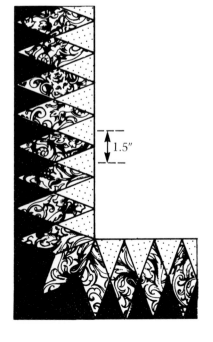

1.5″

that would produce a parallelogram instead of a diamond (fig. 95). If you look at the eight-pointed star (fig. 96), you will see that the colored area is the same as the unit for the border. But how does one know what size star to draft in order to give 4.25″ across the area indicated by the arrow? (This is where high school algebra comes in handy. I think the only use I have made of it since leaving high school is for figuring eight-pointed star borders!)

Because the eight-pointed star cannot be drafted into a grid of squares it is impossible to know immediately what size square one will need. So the first step is to draft an eight-pointed star into any size square. I chose 8½″ and it gave a distance of 3½″ across the area of the border unit. Therefore, using a simple algebraic equation we can now say that 3.5″ is to an 8½″ square as 4.25″ is to X.

$$\frac{3.5}{8.5} = \frac{4.25}{X}$$

To continue working it out you get:

$$3.5X = 8.5 \times 4.25$$
$$3.5X = 36.125$$
$$X = 10.32$$

Now we know that an eight-pointed star will have to be drafted in a 10.32″ square in order to get the correct-sized pattern pieces for the border.

This same procedure can be used with other eight-pointed star designs, or for any border designs for that matter. Let's say you want to use a diamond from the star in the border at left (fig. 97) and in order to fit around the quilt the width across each diamond has to be 1.5″. An 8.5″ star would produce a diamond that is 1⅞″ across its widest point. Therefore 1⅞″ is to an 8.5″ square as 1.5″ is to X.

$$\frac{1⅞}{8.5} = \frac{1.5}{X}$$

$$1.875X = 8.5 \times 1.5$$
$$1.875X = 12.75$$
$$X = 6.8″$$

You would need to draft the star in a 6.8″ square in order to get a diamond that was 1.5″ across.

This may all sound very confusing, but if you read this section several times and practice figuring out some sample borders, it should begin to make sense. I wish I could give you an easy solution to figuring the measurements of borders, but it is one of the more difficult hurdles to overcome in quiltmaking.

Fig. 98.

Drafting Appliqué and Quilted Borders

Drafting designs for quilted or appliqué borders is very much the same as for pieced borders. Basically, a border "unit" has to be planned in a size that, when multiplied, will fit evenly the measurements of both the length and width of the quilt. That border unit should start and stop at the same place, so that no matter how many units need to be linked together, the border will always begin and end the same. A corner unit can then be planned that will link the sides. In an 80″ x 90″ quilt, a 10″ unit could be planned—eight units along the width and nine along the length. If the quilt were 72″ x 84″, a 12″ unit could be planned. Once again, it may not always be possible to find a number that multiplies neatly into both dimensions. If that is the case, find a number as close as possible and fudge a little on two of the sides, making the border unit a little longer or shorter in order to get it to fit the edge of the quilt.

To draft either an appliqué or quilted border the procedure is the same. In the appliqué border shown here (fig. 98), a 10″ unit suits the quilt dimensions of 30″ x 50″ perfectly. Three units fit along one side and five along the other. Plan the corner unit to begin where the other unit stops.

To draft this border unit, cut a piece of paper the length and width of the desired size for the section (fig. 98a). Because the unit is symmetrical, one half of it is the mirror image of the other; so fold the piece of paper in half (fig. 98b) and open it again .

Fig. 98a. Fig. 98b.

Study of this border unit (fig. 98c) shows that if half of it is divided into quarters, the upper right corner and lower left corners are mirror images of each other except for the direction of the leaves. Therefore the next step is to divide the half unit into quarters and draw a half flower and part of a vine with leaves on the upper right square. Using tracing paper, copy the design, flip it over and copy it again in the lower left square. The only thing you will need to do is reverse the direction of the leaves. Next flip the whole half unit over and copy it on the other side and it will be complete. (Fig. 98d).

The corner unit is done similarly. Cut a piece of paper the size for the corner, fold it in half diagonally, and draw half the design. Flip it over and draw the other half on the other side (fig. 98e).

Fig. 98c. 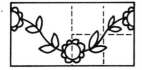 Fig. 98d. Fig. 98e.

Planning any other appliqué or quilted borders would be done in a similar fashion. With either of these two types of borders you will have to plan to draft your own design in order to make it fit around the corners. The chances are slim of finding a ready-made pattern that fits the specific dimensions of your particular quilt. The only way you could use a ready-made border would be to do as suggested earlier and put a different design at the center of each side of the quilt. In the diagram of the quilted border (fig. 99), the garlands on the top and bottom meet the center motif differently from those at the sides. However, it is barely noticeable and not as distracting as having the corners unmatched. To repeat, the main consideration when planning any border is for it to suit the quilt and to flow smoothly, especially at the corners.

Peonies, medallion wall quilt made by Betty Larson in the spring of 1977. Virginia, 45″ square.

Fig. 99.

Spring, medallion quilt made by Alice Geiger, June, 1978-April, 1979. The colors are predominantly purple and beige. The design was inspired by Hawaiian type quiltmaking. Maryland, 95″ square.

Quilting

Quilting should play as large a part in the creation of a beautiful quilt as other workmanship, color and design. First begun out of the need to hold layers of fabrics together and to keep cotton batting in place, quilting evolved into a further expression of the quiltmaker's expertise, design sense and creativity.

In recent years there unfortunately has been a development that, to my mind, has affected the entire look of many quilts and minimized their beauty. The culprit has been polyester batting. It is not that there is anything wrong with that type of batting, but the way it was first presented to the public changed quilting habits. "You no longer need to quilt so closely," quilters were told. "Now you can leave as much as six or eight inches between quilting stitches and there will be no problem with the batting shifting." This type of promotion made many quiltmakers forget that quilting not only holds the layers together, but also enhances the design by adding relief and texture to the quilt surface. Fortunately, many are once again adding more quilting to their projects, having realized that it is an integral part of the design.

Batting

There are several types of batting available. Each has its advantages and disadvantages. You can choose from polyester, cotton or a blend of polyester and cotton. Wool batts are also available from some sources. (With the number of moth holes I have seen in antique wool quilts, a wool batting seems risky.) The use of polyester batting will give a puffier look to the quilting, whereas a cotton or cotton-polyester blend will give a flatter look. No matter what kind of batting is used, the more quilting that is done, the flatter the piece will be. A 100% cotton batting tends to separate and lump after several washings; polyester, or polyester-cotton blends will hold up through repeated washings. The cotton and cotton-polyester blend battings do not have the same problem with fiber migration that the all polyester battings do. (See page 100 for a description of fiber migration.)

To fill a very large quilt you can "splice" two pieces of batting together in the following manner: Use a type of batting that can be separated, and peel back about four inches along the edge of each piece (fig. 100a). Cut off the top of one piece and the bottom of the other and overlap them (fig. 100b). Tack the two pieces together with large stitches (fig. 100c). Splicing the batting in this way eliminates the bulk caused if the two complete layers are simply overlapped, and it will keep the batting from separating.

Fig. 100a.

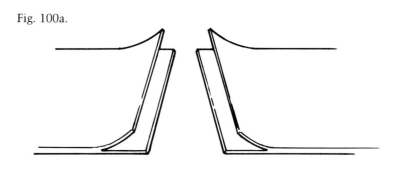

Fig. 100b.

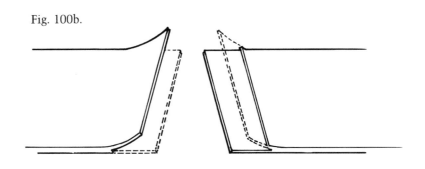

Fig. 100c.

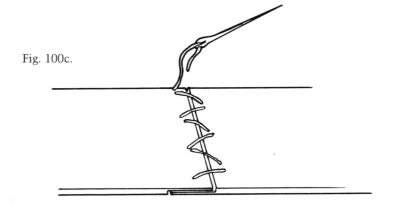

Quilting Thread

There are two main types of quilting thread available—100% cotton and cotton-polyester blend. I prefer the 100% cotton for three reasons. First, cotton thread does not stretch and thus allows a smoother result. A thread of a polyester-cotton blend tends to be elastic. It stretches as it is being pulled taut and then when the quilt is removed from the frame the thread relaxes, causing puckers. The puckering can be particularly bad when a lot of quilting such as stippling is done. To get the smoothest quilting stitches, a piece should be stretched fairly taut in a frame. As the stitches are made, the quilter gives a slight tug on the thread, thus causing the stitches to become tight and look smooth and even. Use of a frame controls the tension so that the stitches are neither pulled too tight nor allowed to be too loose.

Second, I prefer 100% cotton thread because it knots less readily than polyester. And, third, with age it is less apt to cut through the cotton fabric than polyester.

The color of quilting thread to use can vary, depending upon the look that is desired. Sometimes you will want to have the stitches show in sharp contrast to the fabric and at other times you may want them to be unobtrusive and simply blend in. A light thread on a dark fabric may detract from the look of the design. There are no rules saying a certain color must be used. You should choose the color that you feel will look the best. It must also be remembered that stitches may not always look as uniform on the back of the quilt as they do on the front. Therefore you may want to choose backing and quilting thread that are not in sharp contrast to each other. Not all colors are available in quilting-weight thread. A 100% cotton heavy-duty thread can be used as a substitute, and it is usually available in a wide variety of colors.

When a standard quilting thread cannot be found, many people make their thread stronger by pulling it through a piece of beeswax. I have found that thread waxed this way gets sticky and pulls out pieces of batting during the quilting. A way to deal with the stickiness was suggested to me by some Canadian quilters. They said to iron the thread after it is pulled through the beeswax. I envisioned running to the iron every time the thread was waxed! But they suggested cutting several lengths of thread, running them through the wax and then laying them on a piece of tissue paper. The tissue paper is then folded over the thread and all the pieces are ironed at once. This process creates a texture very similar to that of the standard quilting thread and eliminates the stickiness.

Backing

There is a temptation to use sheets for the backing of quilts because they come in such large sizes. Sheets usually have a high thread count, however, and are very difficult to quilt through. I stay away from heavier fabrics and prefer a 100% cotton fabric similar to those used on the front of the quilt. Whether to use a print or plain fabric on the back is a matter of choice. A beautiful paisley or floral may be the perfect backing to complement the colors on the front. However, if you plan to do some fine quilting and want it to stand out on the back, a solid muslin or white will show it off much better.

Usually, two widths of fabric pieced together are large enough for a backing. Rather than one seam straight down the middle, it looks better to have two seams. One width of the fabric will go down the center and the other width will be split—with the two halves going to either side of the center panel. Cut the batting a few inches larger than the quilt top so that if a hoop is used the backing can be folded over the batting to protect it during the quilting process, and also to allow for any possible stretching of the top.

Preparing for Quilting

Before basting the layers of the quilt together, check to be sure that there are no threads hanging on the wrong side. Nothing is worse than to be quilting along and suddenly discover a dark thread showing through the quilt top.

If there are any areas in a quilt with a very light fabric next to a very dark, press the seams towards the dark cloth so that a shadow of the darker fabric will not show through. On my *Ray of Light*, the light and dark *Sawtooth* border created a problem. I knew from the beginning that with such small pieces it would be impossible to press all the seams toward the navy fabric. Therefore, I cut the navy triangles a fraction smaller so that the edges of the blue seam allowance would not show beyond those of the white. The seams of the white triangles acted as a lining for the blue.

If there are any areas in the quilt top where several points come together, clip the excess off the points so they do not form a lump. Do not cut all of the points the same, but taper each differently to ease out the bulkiness.

The Quilting Frame

I am often asked what kind of quilting frame I prefer. What is important is not the *type* but the *use* of some kind of frame. A frame provides tension on the piece so that the quilting stitches can be pulled to the proper degree of tautness. Without a frame the stitches may be pulled either too tightly or not tight enough. I use a large floor frame and find I prefer it over the others. One of the main advantages of a large frame is that it cuts down on handling of the quilt. Less handling is particularly advantageous to a medallion quilt because it helps keep the borders straight. Once a quilt is put in a large frame it can stay there until the quilting is complete, but with a hoop the quilt is constantly being moved in and out.

Some people do not have the space for a large frame or have difficulty sitting comfortably at one. A round or oval hoop can also work satisfactorily. However, a small embroidery hoop should not be used to quilt a large project, because of the excessive handling it entails. It is better to use a round or oval hoop of at least 30″ or a floor-sized frame. I often hear complaints about frames: They produce backaches, they make it difficult to get small stitches, the first stitch is always so much larger than the others, and on and on. I was also discouraged when I started quilting with a frame, and almost gave up. Quilting has a totally different "feel" from other sewing. It does not feel natural. However, it is a learnable skill like knitting or crocheting. It feels awkward at first. But eventually, I can assure you, if you give it time your work will look 100% better when you use a frame than if you do not. It took me one month of quilting at least three hours a day to finally begin to feel comfortable with it. So don't give up.

Basting the Quilt

A medallion quilt must be basted with care. It is important for the many borders to be straight and for the corners to turn squarely. Check often to be sure the borders are not bowed. If they are, pull them out a little or push them in until they are straight.

I usually baste as shown here (fig. 101)—first sewing diagonally from the center and then in grids. I also specifically baste along some of the borders to make sure that they will be straight. I plan to have no more than eight square inches free of basting stitches.

Do not remove any of the basting threads until all of the quilting is complete, otherwise the basting stitches on the outer edges could loosen and cause the borders to become crooked.

Fig. 101.

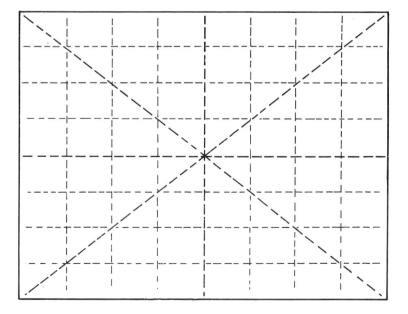

Fig. 102. **Lighthouse Tower** (eight-pointed star category). Designed by Jinny Beyer for the 1981 Sea Pines Seminar.

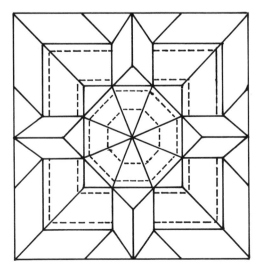

Marking for Quilting

If it is at all possible, I try not to have to mark quilting lines on the fabric. However, there are times when a decorative design needs to be drawn. It can either be marked as you go or before the quilt is basted together. If it is a complicated design, it is probably best to do it ahead of time. I like to use a light table. A very easy way to rig your own is to buy a piece of heavy glass from the hardware store, pull apart a table that has leaves and set the glass over the opening in the table. Put the light on the floor underneath the glass. Draw the design with a bold line on a piece of white paper. Then put the design on the glass and place the fabric over it. Unless a very dark fabric is used, the design should be visible through the fabric. When marking on a light-colored fabric I usually use a hard lead pencil (#3) and press *very* lightly. Check before marking the fabric to be sure the pencil will wash out. On a dark color I use tailor's chalk or a hard soap, broken into splinters. There are a variety of commercial markers available. The main consideration is to choose one that will wash out. I am very wary of the widely acclaimed blue markers that come off with the swipe of a damp cloth. They add a chemical to the cloth, and who knows what kind of reaction it will have in years to come? Furthermore, I have seen disasters created by marks that would not wipe out.

Quilting Design

The quilting should emphasize certain areas and act as a background to others. When quilting around shapes in a design I like to sew about one-quarter inch from the seams just past the seam allowances. This eliminates quilting through the extra fabrics from the seams. If you are not able to "eyeball" the distance, you can use ¼-inch masking tape as a guide. Standard-size Scotch tape can also be used by centering it directly over the seam and quilting on either side of it. There are times when this method might detract from the design. For example, when quilting a pattern such as *Lighthouse Tower* (fig. 102), you might want to emphasize the octagon shape in the center and not the eight triangles that make up the octagon. Instead of making the triangles stand out by quilting around each one, I would emphasize the octagon shape by quilting right along the lines of the design in the fabric border, as shown below. The same would be true in the other area with borders. Almost any time a border stripe is used I quilt along the border, not around the piece.

There are other times when an angular geometric design may give the illusion of curves and you might want to quilt curves to enhance that effect. The main thing is to study your quilt and choose the amount of quilting and type of design that best suits it.

When planning the quilting you may want to consider whether the design is going to run across the straight or

154

Above:

Omaki, pieced, appliquéd, reverse appliquéd and embroidered quilt made by Virginia Suzuki, May, 1978-November, 1979. This is Virginia's Japanese family heritage quilt. It has her family crest in the corners. 84" x 92".

Above right:

Tranquility, appliquéd and pieced medallion quilt made by Kathryn Kuhn, 1980-1981. The central appliqué medallion is an adaptation of one of the motifs in the oriental-style print used in the quilt. The pieced border was inspired by a fence in the same fabric. 85½" x 101½".

Right:

Great Seal Eagle medallion quilt, from the first quarter of the 19th century. (Courtesy of the Smithsonian Institution, Washington D.C.)

Nantucket Compass Medallion, pieced quilt made by Joan Christensen, 1978-1982. The *Mariner's Compass* center, composed of 64 points, reminds Joan of her family's many vacations to Nantucket. The quilted scallop shell is a rubbing of a shell she picked up on the beach. Virginia, 105″ square.

Ribbon of Darkness, pieced medallion quilt made by Mary Ellen Simmons, 1978-1979. The white areas around the center have a beautiful quilted design with stippling for the background. 96″ square.

Ray of Light, medallion quilt made by Jinny Beyer in 1977. The quilt was named after Jinny's daughter, Kiran, who was born while Jinny was living in India. Her Hindi name means Ray of Light. 84″ × 94″.

bias grain of the fabric. Curved and bias designs were used on old quilts so that the stitching did not run along the grain line. Often if the quilting was done along the grain the stitches would become lost in the weave of the fabric. This is not a major consideration with today's more closely woven fabrics, but the idea is worth keeping in mind.

There are apt to be large areas of plain fabric in a medallion quilt that will have to be treated with quilting in some manner. If the plain fabric is a solid color or a subtle print, then some type of decorative quilting pattern can be chosen. Rather than taking a design from a book, why not create your own quilting pattern? Take the design from some part of the quilt top, either a motif printed in one of the fabrics or an echo of one of the pieced or appliquéd designs. I feel it is just as important to have the quilting designs related to each other and to other elements in the top as it is to integrate colors, fabrics and overall design.

My *Ray of Light* quilt has large areas of muslin around the central medallion. I chose to quilt the feather design, a motif taken from the large printed batik fabric that was used in the quilt. (See below.)

Detail showing the batik fabric from which the feather quilting design was taken for **Ray of Light.**

If you are going to use some type of decorative design for a quilting pattern in plain areas, then it is very important that you do not forget the background. The design will not show well if it is quilted alone with no treatment of the background. The quilting must be planned to fill the entire space.

There are various ways to treat the background, depending on the look you want and the amount of quilting you want to do. Diagonal lines, double diagonal lines, cross-hatching, double cross-hatching and clamshell are some traditional background designs that are shown here (fig. 103).

Fig. 103.

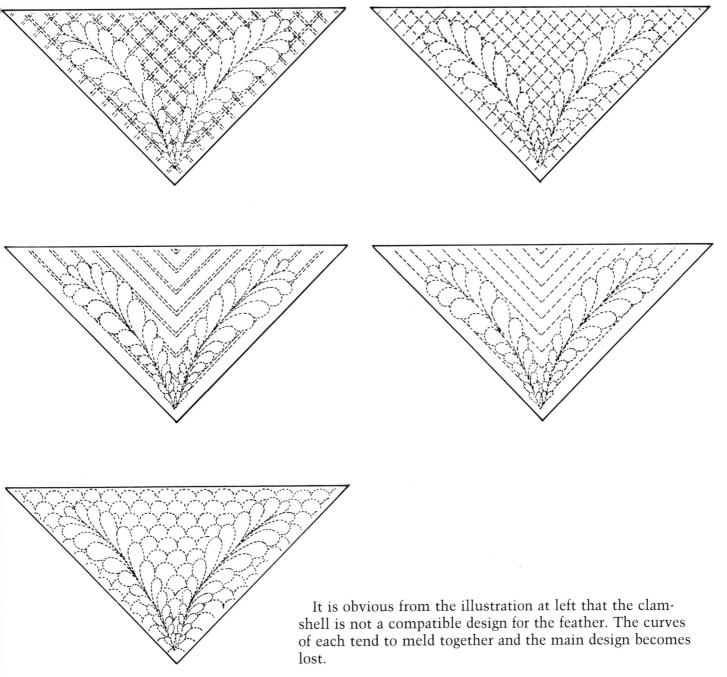

It is obvious from the illustration at left that the clam-shell is not a compatible design for the feather. The curves of each tend to meld together and the main design becomes lost.

It is also possible to use concentric curves, squares or triangles, depending on the shape of the area you are quilting (fig 104). When quilting larger areas, I use masking tape or Scotch tape as guides for straight lines.

Fig. 104.

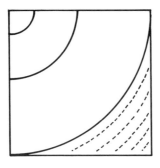 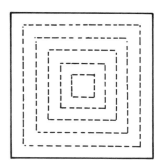

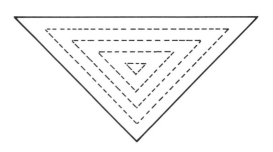

An old type of background quilting today's quiltmakers are rediscovering is stippling (also called meandering or pressed work). This is a technique used in the 18th and early 19th centuries in many of the old "white work" quilts, or others with elaborate quilting. At first glance, one might think that the stitches are taken at random—going this way and that to produce the stippled effect. In fact the quilting is done in waves of rows about $1/16$th of an inch apart going outward from the design. It is similar to Hawaiian quilting except the rows are much closer together. After a few rows are done with tiny stitches, the rows disappear and the stippled effect appears. (See fig. 105 and the photo opposite.) If you try this type of quilting and find that you still see the rows and are not getting a stippled effect, check to make sure your thread is pulled tight. And use a frame if you haven't already. Pulled too tight the work will pucker; if it is not pulled tight enough the thread will just lie on the fabric without creating any relief. To test for the correct tautness of any quilting, put a pin under one of the stitches and pull up on it. If you cannot pull up any extra thread, the tension is probably just right. When there is a lot of excess, the quilting thread has not been pulled hard enough. If you have trouble even getting the pin under the stitch, it is probably too tight.

Fig. 105.

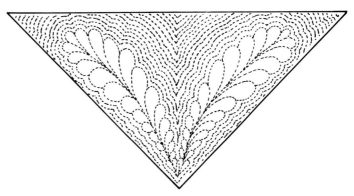

Detail showing stippled quilting on **Ray of Light**.

Delicate quilting designs will not show well on large printed fabrics. The question of how to quilt those areas arises. As discussed earlier, prints with flowing overall designs are probably preferable to those with strict geometrics that might fight with the design of the quilt. Free-flowing prints, on the other hand, make it more difficult to choose an appropriate quilting pattern.

Some people painstakingly quilt around the motifs in the fabric. Although this is beautiful, it may be more work than you want to do. A simple geometric design that can be repeated in all areas where that fabric is used can also be very effective. Perhaps one of the designs suggested as background quilting would work. You will be surprised at how pleasing the regular repeat of a geometric design can be, even on a very patterned fabric.

How to quilt a printed fabric border is another question. Even though there is a lot of extra work involved, I think it is very important to quilt along the design of the printed border. If you used a fabric similar to the one in fig. 106 and quilted in straight lines one-fourth inch from the seam, it would look as though the design had been marked through with a pencil. See how the border design is emphasized when the fabric design is followed with quilting stitches.

Fig. 106.

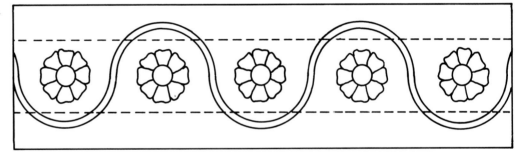

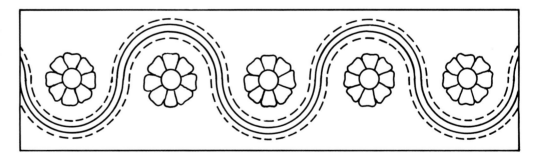

Finishing

When all the quilting is finished, trim the backing and batting even with the edges of the top and add the binding. I prefer using a bias binding cut from one of the darker fabrics used in the quilt. An edging cut from the straight of the fabric is apt to wear out more quickly because of extra stress along the grain lines. A bias has the grain going at an angle to the edge of the quilt so that no one thread gets constant wear. Furthermore, a bias binding gives a smoother finish.

The common way to sew a binding on a quilt is first to stitch the binding to the front side and then turn it to the back, whip-stitching it into place. This method is difficult to use when the final edge of the quilt has a fabric border printed with straight lines. In order to keep the lines straight, I sew the binding on the *wrong* side first, bring it over to the front so I can see the pattern, and sew with invisible stitches right along the line.

The final task should be signing and dating your quilt. We are fortunate to have so many fine examples of historic medallion quilts that help us to understand their role in the evolution of quilt design. However, it is sad that most of their makers remain anonymous, leaving us to wonder who they were. Such exquisite workmanship and fine design deserve recognition.

Two hundred years from now when people look back at *our* quilts, they may speculate as to why there was such a resurgence of interest at this time. Why, in an age of computers, would anyone want to spend so much time making a quilt? We might wish we could be on hand to tell them of the pride we took in our work, the joy we felt in sharing it with others, and the fulfillment of deep needs that quilt-making gave us. If we cannot tell them such things, we can at least sign and date our quilts—so *they* will not wonder who *we* were.

Signature on the back of **Ray of Light.**

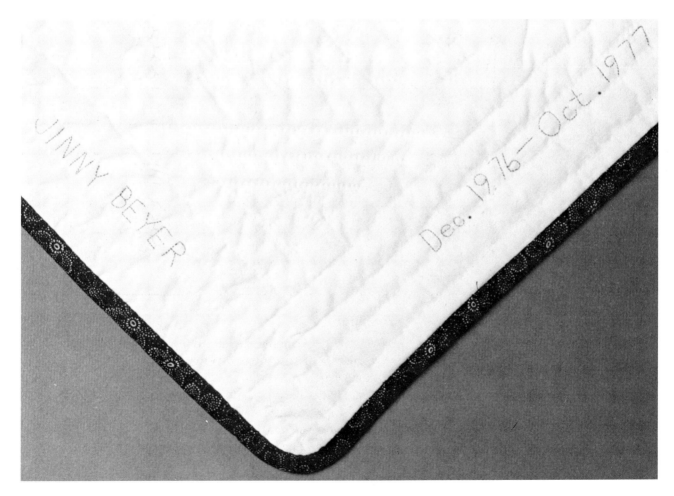

Bowknots and Swags, early 19th century. The swag border is of blue cotton printed with tiny white designs. The center motif is cut from black cotton and handpainted with flowers. The bowknots that tie the swags are made of narrow bands cut from brown and tan printed cotton and are appliquéd to the background. The peacocks in the border have been pieced of various fabrics and then appliquéd. Embroidery adds detail and softness. 89" x 93". (Courtesy of the Shelburne Museum, Shelburne, Vermont.)

Bibliography

Bacon, Lenice. *American Patchwork Quilts.* New York: William Morrow & Co., Inc., 1973.

Baines, Edward. *History of the Cotton Manufacture in Great Britain.* London: H. Fisher, R. Fisher, and P. Jackson, 1835.

Beer, Alice. *Trade Goods.* Washington, D.C.: Smithsonian Institution Press, 1970.

Beyer, Jinny. *The Quilter's Album of Blocks and Borders.* McLean, Virginia: EPM Publications, Inc., 1980.

Beyer, Jinny. *Patchwork Patterns.* McLean, Virginia: EPM Publications, Inc., 1979.

Bishop, Robert. *New Discoveries in American Quilts.* New York: E.P. Dutton & Co., Inc., 1975.

Bishop, Robert, and Safanda, Elizabeth. *A Gallery of Amish Quilts.* New York: E.P. Dutton & Co., Inc., 1976.

Brett, Katharine B. "Chintz, an Influence of the East on the West." *Antiques* 64, no. 6, pp. 480–483.

Brett, Katharine B. "Variants of the Flowering Tree in Indian Chintz." *Antiques,* 77, no. 3, pp. 280–283.

Carlisle, Lillian Baker. *Pieced Work & Appliqué Quilts at Shelburne Museum.* Shelburne, Vermont: The Shelburne Museum, 1957.

Caulfield, S.F.A. and Saward, Blanche C. *The Dictionary of Needlework, An Encyclopedia of Artistic, Plain, and Fancy Needlework.* London: L. Upcott Gill, 1882.

Cirot, J.E. *A Dictionary of Symbols,* 2d ed. Translated from Spanish by Jack Sage. New York: Philosophical Library, Inc., 1962.

Clabburn, Pamela. *The Needleworker's Dictionary.* New York: William Morrow & Co., Inc., 1976.

Defoe, Daniel. *A Plan of the English Commerce.* Great Britain: Shakespeare Head Press, 1927.

Dow, George Francis. *The Arts and Crafts in New England, 1704–1755.* Wayside Press, 1927.

Finley, Ruth E. *Old Patchwork Quilts and the Women Who Made Them.* Philadelphia: J.B. Lippincott Co., 1929.

Hall, Carrie A., and Kretsinger, Rose G. *The Romance of the Patchwork Quilt in America.* New York: The Caxton Printers, Ltd., 1935.

Holstein, Jonathan. *The Pieced Quilt, An American Design Tradition.* Greenwich, Connecticut: New York Graphic Society, Ltd.,1973.

Home Arts Studio Patterns. Des Moines, Iowa: ca. 1930-1940.

Illuminations, Inc. Mandala Calendar. Sommerville, Mass.: 1979.

Irwin, John. "Origins of 'Oriental' Chintz Design." *Antiques* 75, no. 1, pp. 84–86.

Irwin, John. "Origins of the Oriental Style in English Decorative Art." *Burlington Magazine* 96, no. 625, pp. 106–114.

Irwin, John. "Indian Textile Trade in the 17th Century." *Journal of Indian Textile History,* numbers I-IV (1955–1959).

Irwin, John, and Brett, Katharine B. *Origins of Chintz.* London: Her Majesty's Stationery Office, 1970.

Irwin, John, and Hall, Margaret. *Indian Painted and Printed Fabrics.* vol. 1. Ahmedabad: S.R. Bastihar on Behalf of the Calico Museum of Textiles, Ahmedabad.

Katzenberg, Dena S. *Blue Traditions.* Baltimore: The Baltimore Museum of Art, 1973.

Mailey, Jean. "Indian Textiles in the Museum's Collections." *Chronicle of the Museum for the Arts of Decoration of the Cooper Union* 2, no. 5.

Montgomery, Florence. *Printed Textiles.* New York: The Viking Press, 1970.

Orlofsky, Patsy and Myron. *Quilts in America.* New York: McGraw-Hill Book Co., 1974.

Parry, John W. *The Story of Spices.* New York: Chemical Publishing Co., Inc., 1953.

Pettit, Florence. *America's Printed & Painted Fabrics 1600–1900.* New York: Hastings House, Publishers, 1970.

Rosengarten, Frederic, Jr. *The Book of Spices.* Wynnewood, Pennsylvania: The Livingston Publishing Co., 1969.

Safford, Carleton L., and Bishop, Robert. *America's Quilts and Coverlets.* New York: E.P. Dutton & Co., Inc., 1972.

Webster, Marie D. *Quilts, Their Story and How to Make Them.* New York: Doubleday, Page & Co., 1915.

Index